LIFEWORDS
A Prophetic Life Daily Devotional

by Ed Traut

Copyright © 2014 Ed Traut

All rights reserved. Except as permitted under the U.S. Copyright Act of 1976, no part of this publication may be reproduced, distributed, or transmitted in any form or by any means, or stored in a database or retrieval system, without the prior written permission of the publisher.

Prophetic Life Publishing

18830 Salado Canyon
San Antonio, TX 78258

Visit our website at propheticlife.com

Printed in the United States of America

First Edition: March 2014

ISBN-13: 978-1496033116

Foreword

In Genesis we read how that the Lord came every day to fellowship with Adam and Eve. By the mere frequency of His visit we can see that God wants to visit and fellowship with us daily. It wasn't a long period of the day, it was only a slice of the twenty four period that Adam and Eve experienced as the world turned on it's axis.

The Word of God says in the "cool" of the day, showing that it was a time that was conducive and workable for Adam and Eve so that they could get the maximum benefit out of this relationship and fellowship.

It has always been my complete conviction and heart's desire that all children of God should fellowship with God as He created us for that very purpose. In my effort to help my brethren, and myself, to walk in fellowship with the Lord I generated this devotional which is available to sign up for on our website. It is daily fresh manna and thoughts from the King to our hearts, illuminating scripture and making the Word of God alive to us, strengthening our daily relationship with Him.

LifeWords is a daily devotional that just takes a minute to read but can change your entire day, and even your life, if you take the time to dwell on it and develop a habit of fellowship and spending time with the King of Kings.

We trust that this daily devotional book will be a blessing to you as it has been to myself and many others.

January 1

Revelation 21:5
"He who was seated on the throne said, "I am making everything new!" Then he said, "Write this down, for these words are trustworthy and true." NIV

> Let us always keep in mind that He is "seated on the throne". He remains sovereign and Lord of all.
>
> God is making everything new! As we begin the new year the Lord Himself will renew all things.
>
> He told the angel to write it down and make a note of it because no matter how it looks or how strange the world seems right now, the Lord is not only in control, He is refreshing and doing something brand new.

Father, I praise You for the fact that You are King of Kings and Lord of Lords and on the throne. I ask that You refresh my heart and strengthen my soul that I may embrace this new year with excitement knowing that You are making all things new. Amen!

January 2

Acts 3:6
"Then Peter said, "Silver or gold I do not have, but what I have I give you. In the name of Jesus Christ of Nazareth, walk."" NIV

God's idea of and for the encounters in our lives are often very different to our own perceptions.

We have something from Him that we need to share. He has given us giftings and anointings for each encounter God has planned for us in our lives.

We ought to be attentive to the situations and be led by the spirit each time.

Prayer: Father lead me today by your spirit to be effective and fruitful for your kingdom and your name's sake. Thank you for the anointing and gifts in my life. Help me to function in them according to your will. Amen.

January 3

Mark 5:34
'He said to her, "Daughter, your faith has healed you. Go in peace and be freed from your suffering."' NIV

It was not the garment or the touching that healed her but rather her faith. Faith releases the power of God in our lives.

The Lord wants us to enjoy the benefits of what He has for us - and that is why He told her 'you are free from your suffering'.

He called her daughter because she really believed in Him and really had faith in Him.

Prayer: Lord, I pray that You help me eradicate all the doubt in my life that faith may arise and that I may become fruitful in my daily walk with You through faith. Amen.

January 4

Colossians 3:10
"Put on your new nature, and be renewed as you learn to know your Creator and become like him." NLT

We are a new creation and therefore ought to behave in a new way, with a new DNA and nature of whom we are created in the image of - our Lord Jesus.

It is so easy to slip into the old nature's behavior that we are so used to. It takes conscious effort and discipline to choose to behave in our new born again nature.

"Becoming like Him" is an ongoing process and it takes deliberate effort to follow Him and to allow Him to work in our lives.

Prayer: Lord I pray that you help me to put on a new nature today and every day that I can become like You. My desire is to reflect You in all I do. Amen.

January 5

Psalms 74:17
"It was you who set all the boundaries of the earth; you made both summer and winter." NIV

> God is sovereign - He is in control and we need to remind ourselves of this.
>
> There are boundaries and natural elements that we are subject to and we need to recognize that it is just life and do not need to spiritualize everything.
>
> We are fortunate and blessed to be a child of God, who has made all the boundaries.

Prayer: Lord, thank you for your salvation and that I am your child. Give me the wisdom to discern between what is just natural life elements and the spiritual things that are taking place around me. Amen.

January 6

1 John 4:7
"Dear friends, let us love one another, for love comes from God. Everyone who loves has been born of God and knows God." NIV

> No question - Real love comes only from God. He is love.
>
> We need to express that love to each other. Especially to those that seem to be underserving, to qualify us as someone who reflects the Lord.
>
> We are born of God and therefore function in love. If we are struggling we ought to strengthen our connection with Him that His love can flow through us.

Prayer: Father, I praise you today for the love you have for me and for the love you express to me through people. Let your love flow through me that I may be a vessel of this magnificent trait you so reflect. Amen.

January 7

Matthew 6:6
" But when you pray, go into your room, close the door and pray to your Father, who is unseen. Then your Father, who sees what is done in secret, will reward you." NIV

> Prayer is an essential part of our christian life and ought to be taken seriously.
>
> Prayer is something personal and between us and God and needs to be developed into a habit and a way of life.
>
> What we do before the Lord in secret is seen by God. We can expect a reward!

Prayer: Father I thank you for your love towards me. I pray for a spirit of prayer to continually rest on me that I can be a person of prayer everyday and frequently. Teach me your heart and ways to pray. Amen.

January 8

Mark 5:36 "Ignoring what they said, Jesus told the synagogue ruler, "Don't be afraid; just believe." NIV

> Often, to exercise our faith, we have to absolutely ignore what people say because their words can create fear and doubt.
>
> Jesus spoke words to the synagogue ruler. Words will either create faith or damage faith through fear.
>
> He told him not to be afraid - fear is the direct contrast to faith. He said, just believe.

Prayer: Lord I want to just believe, so I ask you to help me to have a constant guard over what I hear and listen to that I may follow your way of faith and not be influenced by man to contradict the faith you have put into my heart. Amen.

January 9

Jeremiah 11:4 "Obey me and do everything I command you, and you will be my people, and I will be your God." NIV

God wants us to obey Him. Obedience is something we have to cultivate continually as our minds often stand against what we don't understand when we have received instructions from the Lord.

DO - doing God's word and doing everything He commands is what the Lord requires of us.

He promised Israel that obedience would ensure His relationship towards them and it is not just by this promise and by His grace that we obey and do His will but because we love Him.

Prayer: Father I pray that I hear what you say and obey you. Give me the grace to do all that you ask of me and to respond to you immediately. My heart desires to follow after you as I trust you fully. Amen.

January 10

1 John 1:9 "If we confess our sins, he is faithful and just and will forgive us our sins and purify us from all unrighteousness." NIV

Simply confessing will render forgiveness from the Lord.

We can expect to be purified in every way when we confess because He is faithful and just.

The completed work of Christ on the cross was to bring us back to right standing and any failings just need to be confessed to Him.

Prayer: Lord I thank you for this amazing completed work of calvary through Jesus Christ. I thank you and receive my full forgiveness and all that He died for. I pray that you help me to walk in uprightness in every way to continue to grow and become more like you. Amen.

January 11

John 16:14 "He will bring glory to me by taking from what is mine and making it known to you." NIV

> The Lord will always glorify Jesus. Whenever we see the Holy Ghost function or anything that happens, it always glorifies the Lord. If not, then we have to question where it comes from.
>
> The Holy Spirit takes what is the Lord's and reveals it to us. It is an ongoing daily process to receive revelation as we grow in the Lord.
>
> In our daily walk with Him we should desire more of Him and the Holy Ghost is there to reveal it to us.

Prayer: Father, I thank you for Jesus and for this amazing salvation. Help me to continue to hunger and thirst for righteousness and your ways. Lord I desire to know you even more. Amen.

January 12

Matthew 18:19 "Again, I tell you that if two of you on earth agree about anything you ask for, it will be done for you by my Father in heaven." NIV

A profound promise and truth - if we can just get two or three to agree!

It takes sincerity and unity of heart to form an agreement with some one else, and then faith to believe it will happen.

Getting someone to agree with our request, not only unites faith to bring about a miracle, but also is able to release God's power through unity.

Prayer: Father I thank you for this promise, and ask that you lead us and teach us to utilize this truth effectively. Give me someone to pray in agreement with today. Amen.

January 13

2 Peter 3:18 "But grow in the grace and knowledge of our Lord and Savior Jesus Christ. To him be glory both now and forever! Amen." NIV

We ought to grow continually in the Lord Jesus.

To grow in this grace of our Lord is not only unique and phenomenal but life changing in us and those around us.

Growing in the knowledge of the Lord requires walking with Him, pursuing Him and being hungry and thirsty after Him.

Prayer: Father I ask you to allow me to grow in this grace and knowledge of our Lord. I long to become more like you and to know you in every way. Amen.

January 14

1 Peter 5:7 " Give all your worries and cares to God, for he cares about you." NLT

It takes a very conscious effort to give your concerns to God. We often give it but take it back with us. We need to leave it there.

We have cares and worries that trouble us every day and when one is resolved, the next one comes so we need to focus on the Lord and not our troubles.

We can depend upon Him to take care of us and so if we just let Him have all our cares and not stress about our troubles we can walk with trouble-free joy and likeness - this is what God longs for us.

Prayer: Lord, let your joy and peace be my portion today so I will not be concerned and carry burdens and worries. Teach me how to continually give you all my burdens and concerns so that I don't worry but have a worry free life in You and express it to others. Amen.

January 15

Proverbs 11:30 "The seeds of good deeds become a tree of life; a wise person wins friends." NLT

> Even the smallest good deed will evolve and grow into something good - "a tree of life"
>
> When we do good works they do not go unnoticed by the Lord and not only does He reward them but they are ongoing fruit in time to come.
>
> Often through good deeds we win friends wisely; even neighbors and people who are not saved are touched and influenced by even the smallest act of kindness.

Prayer: Lord, make me conscious of being kind and doing good deeds even to people that I am not in close association with to express your kindness and love to produce a tree of life in them and in myself. Amen.

January 16

Exodus 33:15 "Then Moses said to him, "If your Presence does not go with us, do not send us up from here." NIV

> More than anything we need His presence in all we do.
>
> No power, no deliverance, no blessing or provision could ever substitute for the presence of God.
>
> It is better for us to stay where His presence is then to go where we want or long to go.

Prayer: Lord I do desire Your presence and Your anointing in my life. Help me to continue to pursue You and Your presence today. Amen.

January 17

1 Samuel 16:7 "But the Lord said to Samuel, 'Do not consider his appearance or his height, for I have rejected him. The Lord does not look at the things man looks at. Man looks at the outward appearance, but the Lord looks at the heart.'" NIV

God looks at things differently than the way we look at them. His value system is not like ours and we ought to work with His because He sees the motivation of our hearts.

We often judge people and situations by what we see, when we rather need to have God's understanding what really is going on.

We need to ensure that our hearts are always right with Him and the way He wants it to be so that when He looks at our hearts He is satisfied and pleased.

Prayer: Father create in me a clean and contrite heart to do what is right because I know You look at my heart. Help me not to judge from the outside but to evaluate in conjunction with your voice in all situations. Amen.

January 18

Matthew 10:32 "Whoever acknowledges me before men, I will also acknowledge him before my Father in heaven." NIV

We cannot be embarrassed or ashamed to be associated or identified with Jesus. Often we are in situations where acknowledging Him is uncomfortable and owning up might even cost us something.

It is our call and responsibility to preach Christ and acknowledging Him to people so that they are aware that we represent Him.

Acknowledging Him before the world holds us accountable to live for Him and the way He wants us to live to represent Him.

Prayer: Lord Jesus I acknowledge you as my Lord and Savior and I never want to be ashamed or embarrassed of this before anyone at any time. Give me the grace Lord to be obedient to You and to acknowledge you in the most effective way at all times. Amen

January 19

Romans 5:3 "Not only so, but we also glory in our sufferings, because we know that suffering produces perseverance; perseverance, character; and character, hope." NIV

It seems so odd to rejoice in suffering - we are not rejoicing for or because of suffering but in it.

The benefit of suffering is that it will produce perseverance or character that helps us to be fruitful for the Lord in the future in every given situation.

God is focused on eternal matters as we are training here on earth for reigning with Him in eternity.

Prayer: Lord help me to make the most of difficulties and sufferings I have to go through as life presents them to me that I may be effective and grow for your kingdom's sake. Amen.

January 20

Philippians 2:14-15 "Do everything without complaining or arguing, so that you may become blameless and pure, children of God without fault in a crooked and depraved generation, in which you shine like stars in the universe." NIV

> We all struggle with complaining when things are less than desirable but arguing and complaining is not conducive for christian growth.
>
> We will become blameless, pure children of God when we make it a habit and effort not to do this.
>
> It will cause us to stand out and shine in the world if we do not behave this way. We ought to pursue this lifestyle through no arguing and complaining.

Prayer: Lord I thank you for your love and kindness towards me. I ask you to fill me with your joy, peace and an attitude of not complaining or arguing that I can be a daily reflection of you. Thank you for your strengthening for I am unable to it on my own. Amen.

January 21

James 2:13 "There will be no mercy for those who have not shown mercy to others. But if you have been merciful, God will be merciful when he judges you." NLT

> God's judgment is imminent for all.
>
> God is merciful and requires us to be merciful too.
>
> We have daily opportunities to show mercy to people around us in various circumstances - let's show mercy!

Prayer: Father, I thank you for your great mercy and grace you have shown me. I ask that you give me wisdom and the right heart attitude to show mercy to people around me. Amen.

January 22

John 7:37 ""Anyone who is thirsty may come to me! Anyone who believes in me may come and drink! For the Scriptures declare, 'Rivers of living water will flow from his heart.'" NLT

And open invitation to all to come and get all that you need from Jesus; but it takes coming to the Lord.

Nothing in this world can quench our thirst like the Lord.

Then there is a promise that as we come to drink we become a river that flows inside of us out to others. So we get quenched and we become a source.

Prayer: Lord Jesus, I thank you for the invitation to come and drink. I drink from you and look toward you for all my desires and needs. I pray that you help me to be a source to others today. Amen.

January 23

Jude 1:20 "But you, dear friends, build yourselves up in your most holy faith and pray in the Holy Spirit." NIV

> We are called to build each other up - not criticize or tear one another down.
>
> When we build each other up it should stimulate and strengthen our faith and confidence in the Lord Jesus.
>
> When we pray in the power of the Holy Spirit we are far more effective than just crying from a need, but allowing the Spirit to pray through us and for us.

Prayer: Father, I ask you to give me the grace to strengthen my brother in faith as we journey together spiritually. I ask you to help me to continue to pray in the Spirit and by the Spirit. Amen.

January 24

Hebrews 4:16 "Let us then approach the throne of grace with confidence, so that we may receive mercy and find grace to help us in our time of need." NIV

>Let us remember that the throne that God sits on is embellished with grace.
>
>Because of His grace we don't scour but come to Him with confidence and expectancy regardless of how we see ourselves and in what state of spiritual success we are in.
>
>When we approach His throne with confidence we can expect to receive mercy and grace in our time of need, regardless of our shortcomings. We can be bold in our expectancies.

Prayer: Lord I thank your for your grace and mercy and I come boldly today because of it. When I pray I do expect you to help me in my time of need. You are a God that answers prayer and I thank you for that. Amen.

January 25

Matthew 21:22 "If you believe, you will receive whatever you ask for in prayer." NIV

It is up to us - "if" we believe we will receive.

Our struggle is with unbelief and fear that the devil uses to try and diminish our faith. We must watch out for doubt and unbelief.

It is "whatever" we ask for in prayer - there is no limit, there are no conditions. So let us then ask, and work on believing without fear or doubt.

Prayer: Father I thank you for the promise Jesus gave me that I will receive whatever I ask for if I believe. Help me to overcome all fear and unbelief that I may have confidence when I ask. Amen.

January 26

Joshua 1:9 "Have I not commanded you? Be strong and courageous. Do not be terrified; do not be discouraged, for the Lord your God will be with you wherever you go." NV

> It is a command to be strong and courageous - which insinuates we have reason because of what we face to be perhaps threatened or full of fear.
>
> The enemy tries to terrify and discourage us but we are commanded not to be either.
>
> The Lord will be with us where ever we go - we have this confidence that when we embark on a new journey or face a challenge, He will be with us.

Prayer: Lord I thank You as You were with Joshua and the promise You made him, so You will it be with me today and in my future where ever I go. I expect it and by Your help and grace I will not have fear or terror. I will trust in You because of Your faithfulness. Amen.

January 27

James 1:6-8 "But when he asks, he must believe and not doubt, because he who doubts is like a wave of the sea, blown and tossed by the wind. That man should not think he will receive anything from the Lord; he is a double-minded man, unstable in all he does." NIV

> So we must ask without wavering or fear of unbelief - it is the enemy's concentrated effort to try and put a little bit of doubt and fear in us. He tried to cause Eve to doubt by saying "Did God really say?".
>
> If we have fear or doubt we are nothing but a wave tossed around with no clear direction or purpose and then we are told we will receive nothing!
>
> If we have doubts and fears we are unstable - and that is not how God has planned our original paths.

Prayer: Father, I thank you for all you do and all you have done. Help me to overcome doubt and fear that I will not be tossed to and fro like a wave but be stable in every way, believing and trusting in you regardless of what I see or do. Amen.

January 28

Isaiah 40:31 "but those who hope in the Lord will renew their strength. They will soar on wings like eagles; they will run and not grow weary, they will walk and not be faint." NIV

We put our hope (which is positive expectancy) in the Lord and we are refreshed and renewed - often we are weary from challenges and battles and this is our confidence that we will be renewed.

Soaring on wings like eagles and not getting tired or weary is all an attribute and promise as we seek the Lord or look to the Lord for our renewal of strength. Running and not getting tired means that we are going to keep going but we will not be affected by the things that often come against us or obstacles of life.

We need to make a concentrated effort to seek and to hope in the Lord that our strength can constantly be renewed and we will not faint or give up!

Prayer: Lord I thank You for renewing my strength as I wait upon You and look to You. I am weak but I know You are strong in me and I rejoice in that! Amen.

January 29

1 Peter 2:9 "But you are a chosen people, a royal priesthood, a holy nation, a people belonging to God, that you may declare the praises of him who called you out of darkness into his wonderful light." NIV

To be chosen means that God picked us for a specific purpose! He picked us.

We are a people that belong to Him for the purpose of declaring what God has done. Transformed us from, what seemed to be disastrous, into victorious and something to be displayed before man.

Of all that God has created throughout the universe and galaxies, even all the people on the earth, we, the redeemed, are the specific ones He chose and we ought to recognize and rejoice in this enormous privilege and blessing.

Prayer: Lord I thank you for this wonderful salvation and your love for me. Help me to grow and become all that you desire me to be that I may represent you in every way and form. I bless you today and thank you for choosing me. Amen.

January 30

James 4:17 "Anyone, then, who knows the good he ought to do and doesn't do it, sins." NIV

> The moment we receive light and information from the Lord we become responsible for what we learn from Him.
>
> The sin of omission is as severe as the sin we commit.
>
> We ought to take it seriously when the Lord teaches us and grow us to be responsible to obey Him in all things that He enlightens us.

Prayer: Father I thank you that you are the Lord of light and that Your word teaches me and enlightens me. Help me to obey and do all that You ask of me that I will not sin against You by mere omission or even committing things that are wrong. Thank You for Your grace today. Amen.

January 31

James 1:5 "If any of you lacks wisdom, he should ask God, who gives generously to all without finding fault, and it will be given to him." NIV

Wisdom is from God and not easily acquired naturally.

We may gain knowledge but still have no wisdom. Wisdom helps us execute knowledge and to do the right thing.

God gives generally and not sparingly so we can expect God to respond when we ask for wisdom in every situation.

When we gain wisdom from God it not only effects our lives, but the lives of people around us.

Prayer: Father I do ask for wisdom today. I need you and cannot do this by myself. Without you I am nothing so I ask for your wisdom in making the right decisions and to do what is right before you. Amen.

February 1

Isaiah 41:13 "For I am the Lord, your God, who takes hold of your right hand and says to you, Do not fear; I will help you." NIV

> The Lord is our God unconditionally and we belong to Him.
>
> No matter what we are facing or where we seem to go into unseen territory He takes our hand and guides us - that's why we trust Him!
>
> He promises to help us - so often we try to work out solutions of "how" He is going to help us but God's methods are so far above our ways.

Prayer: Thank you Lord that you are my God and that you promise to help me. I put my trust in you today and look to the future with hope and expectancy. Amen.

February 2

James 2:8 "If you really keep the royal law found in Scripture, "Love your neighbor as yourself," you are doing right." NIV

Jesus said that this law is as great as the first law - to love the Lord our God.

Your neighbor encompasses everyone and we ought to love them and regard them as much as we would regard ourselves.

This principle, how we treat each other, is very important to God and we ought to pay careful attention in general to friends, unsaved people and everyone we meet. To treat them with the same principle that God has given us here.

Prayer: Father I thank you that you love me and that you are love. Help me to see all people (neighbors around me) the way you do and treat them with love and kindness. Give me the grace and wisdom always in these situations. Amen.

February 3

2 Timothy 1:7 "For God has not given us a spirit of fear and timidity, but of power, love, and self-discipline." NLT

> We have received this spirit of God which brings positive power and love to us.
>
> All fear has its origin from another source other than God - namely the devil.
>
> Fear does not belong near or in us.
>
> We have a self-controlled and sound mind that we take every thought captive and do not allow our minds to ramble on with thoughts of negative fear.

Prayer: Father I thank you that you have not given me a spirit of fear and I receive the spirit of love and sound mind and self-control. Help me Lord to walk in a defeating attitude towards all attempts of fear and intimidation the enemy brings. I thank you for your strength for you are my strength. Amen.

February 4

Hebrews 13:16 "And do not forget to do good and to share with others, for with such sacrifices God is pleased." NIV

It is in the heart of man to want to please God and we look for ways to do that.

We are reminded to do good and to share - we must be sensitive to the need of others.

It was always God's heart that we treat one another with kindness and in doing so we please the Lord. It is considered a sacrifice.

Prayer: Lord I thank you for all you have done for me and still are doing. Help me to be sensitive to the needs of others and help me to be kind to others. In Jesus name, Amen.

February 5

Romans 4:19 "Without weakening in his faith, he faced the fact that his body was as good as dead—since he was about a hundred years old—and that Sarah's womb was also dead." NIV

> Facing facts means we cling to the truth!
>
> Not wavering in your faith - means not to be moved by the facts or what we see, but solely dependent on what God had said.
>
> The facts often are almost opposite to the truth or what we have heard from the Lord's promises and it is the plan of the devil to help us waiver in faith by looking at the circumstances.

Prayer: Father, help me to keep my eyes and heart focused on what you said and not in what I see. Amen.

February 6

Philippians 1:6 "being confident of this, that he who began a good work in you will carry it on to completion until the day of Christ Jesus." NIV

> God began a good work in us.
>
> He will complete this ongoing process of working and growing us.
>
> We can be confident of God's faithfulness in working in our lives with a specific goal in mind. We ought not to stress when we falter because God will complete it.

Prayer: Lord I thank you that you have begun a good work in me. I surrender to your work and dealings that I can work towards that which you want to perfect in me. Amen.

February 7

Psalm 139:1-3 "O Lord, you have searched me and you know me. You know when I sit and when I rise; you perceive my thoughts from afar. You discern my going out and my lying down; you are familiar with all my ways." NIV

> There is nothing hidden from God about me.
>
> We often get so busy with our schedules in our daily lives that we forget to be mindful of the Lord and His dealings in our lives - He's very attentive and involved in every moment of our lives.
>
> There is nothing we can hide from God so we need to always be open and truthful because He knows everything about us - and cares.

Prayer: Lord I thank you that you do know me and that my heart is completely exposed to you. Teach me your ways that I may grow in you and do all that is pleasing in your site. Amen.

February 8

Habakkuk 3:17 "Even though the fig trees have no blossoms, and there are no grapes on the vines; even though the olive crop fails, and the fields lie empty and barren; even though the flocks die in the fields, and the cattle barns are empty, yet I will rejoice in the Lord! I will be joyful in the God of my salvation!" NLT

> There are seasons in life that we go through that seem to be barren and empty.
>
> It is harder to praise the Lord when things seem so difficult but God is not changed.
>
> In the state of difficulties and challenges we rejoice in the Lord for He is our salvation!

Prayer: Lord, today I lift my eyes to you and rejoice even in the dry seasons of my life. You are my salvation and I will always be glad in you. By your grace, Amen.

February 9

Isaiah 30:18 "Yet the Lord longs to be gracious to you; he rises to show you compassion. For the Lord is a God of justice. Blessed are all who wait for him!" NIV

> It is the nature and heart of God that wants to show us kindness and grace. He picks us up in the worst of circumstances.
>
> He is a God of justice and He measures what is right and not the opinion of man, but to His own holiness.
>
> We are blessed when we wait on Him rather than people. Sometimes He seems slower but His time is always perfect.

Prayer: Lord I thank you that you long to show me grace and want to be kind to me. I am grateful for your grace and your justice. Today I purpose in my heart to look to you as my entire source of life. Amen.

February 10

1 Peter 1:8-9 "Though you have not seen him, you love him; and even though you do not see him now, you believe in him and are filled with an inexpressible and glorious joy, for you are receiving the goal of your faith, the salvation of your souls." NIV

> It is by faith that we are saved and by faith that we serve and get to know Him.
>
> We are filled with a joy that is unable to be explained.
>
> The goal of our faith is salvation and spending eternity with Him.

Prayer: Father I thank you for this wonderful salvation and that you are so real to me. I thank you also that you chose me and died for me, a sinner. It is with great joy and excitement that I serve you because you are so faithful and wonderful! Amen.

February 11

Matthew 28:20 "And surely I am with you always, to the very end of the age." NIV

The Lord said He would never leave us again, ever, after He was on earth. He sent us the comforter/Holy Spirit to be with us until He comes to get us.

There are so many things in life that make us feel lonely and we sometimes have difficulty sensing His presence during those times - but we can be assured that He is there with us.

It is with confidence, regardless our shortcomings and failings, that He will never leave or forsake us. He will be with us till the very end.

Prayer: Lord I thank you for your promises that I will never be alone. I lean on you today , knowing that regardless how I feel or what things look like, you are here with me and will never forsake me. Praise the Lord! Amen.

February 12

Psalms 51:12 "Restore to me the joy of your salvation and grant me a willing spirit, to sustain me." NIV

> Sometimes, through life's ups and downs, we lose some of that joy that we received at our salvation - we need to ask for it to be restored.
>
> The joy of the Lord is a strength in all times and in all circumstances.
>
> A willing spirit to keep us going is the prayer of the writer of Psalms 51's heart - and ours.

Prayer: Father I thank you for this salvation and your joy that is my strength. I ask today that you give me a willing spirit to give me the strength, for I am weak but you are strong in me when I am weak. Amen.

February 13

Luke 10:19 "I have given you authority to trample on snakes and scorpions and to overcome all the power of the enemy; nothing will harm you." NIV

Jesus has given us, not some, but ALL authority to metaphorically trample on snakes and scorpions.

The enemy who is the devil, who comes at us in so many forms, has been defeated and He has given us complete power over him.

Jesus promises that nothing will harm us - we must cling and believe that promise.

Prayer: Father I thank you for our Lord Jesus and I thank you that you have given me all authority over the enemy. Help me to believe it and exercise my authority over the enemy and all he tries to do that I may have power over him and he cannot harm me or my household. I give you thanks for it. Amen.

February 14

Song of Solomon 2:10 "My lover spoke and said to me, "Arise, my darling, my beautiful one, and come with me." NIV

> We have a permanent invitation for intimacy with our Lord.
>
> There is no greater valentine than the Lord. "For no greater love has the man who lays down his love."
>
> The joy and deep satisfaction of any heart can only be found with intimacy with our Lord when we take the time to be with Him.

Prayer: Lord I praise you for your goodness and love. Thank you that your love is unfailing and that it is so consistent in every way. I love you Lord and put you first in my life above all else. Amen.

February 15

Colossians 4:2 "Devote yourselves to prayer, being watchful and thankful." NIV

It is an attitude of heart to be devoted to prayer. It should be our first response in any given situation.

To be watchful and to watch continually is to be alert and mindful to spiritual activity around us as we are spirit beings living in a body with a soul.

Thankfulness - without it we cannot enter the courts of God or even keep a humble heart. We ought to practice thankfulness daily.

Prayer: Lord I pray for your strengthening today that I may be devoted to prayer as a lifestyle and continually watch and be alert to all things around me. I am thankful for all you do and I praise you. Amen.

February 16

2 Peter 3:18 "But grow in the grace and knowledge of our Lord and Savior Jesus Christ. To him be glory both now and forever! Amen." NIV

Grace is something we will grow in - the undeserved favor and enjoyment of His continual mercy.

As we grow in the knowledge and relationship with the Lord Jesus, our lives will be enriched. We ought to keep seeking Him.

We cannot stay stationary in our spiritual walk but must continually grow in all aspects with our Lord.

Prayer: Lord I thank you for your goodness and salvation. I ask you to give me the grace and ability to continue to grow in you and to seek you that I may be fruitful and hear "well done" when I see you face to face. Amen.

February 17

1 Peter 1:13 "Therefore, prepare your minds for action; be self-controlled; set your hope fully on the grace to be given you when Jesus Christ is revealed." NIV

Our minds are being washed daily by the Word of God, but we need to prepare our thought patterns. We do this by what we feed out minds and allow our thoughts to dwell on.

Self-control is a fruit of the Spirit and develops the more we 'walk in the Spirit' (Romans 8:4) and make an effort to practice this discipline.

Our positive expectancy (hope) is in the undeserved favor (grace) that we will receive when we see our blessed savior face to face.

Prayer: Father, I pray for Your help to keep my mind always prepared for action and develop true self control so that I may be effective daily for You! Amen.

February 18

Ephesians 3:19 "May you experience the love of Christ, though it is too great to understand fully. Then you will be made complete with all the fullness of life and power that comes from God." NLT

It is a blessing to be able to "experience" the love of the Lord. We often resist God's love because we feel undeserving but the Lord desires that we embrace it.

The enormity of God's love is beyond man's normal understanding.

There is a major input from God's love and grasping His love brings completeness and fullness in the Lord.

Prayer: Father, I am so grateful for your love that never fails. I embrace it today regardless of how I feel because I know that you do not change. I ask that you open my understanding and enlighten me that I may grasp some of this great love and be comfortable in it. Amen.

February 19

John 10:16 "I have other sheep, too, that are not in this sheepfold. I must bring them also. They will listen to my voice, and there will be one flock with one shepherd." NLT

It is always enlightening for those that serve the Lord to remember that there are others that the Lord use that are not always in the same sphere as we are -spiritually, emotionally or in doctrine.

The Lord wants to unite them and bring them into the same faith fold as we are and we should be attentive to aid the Lord.

The mark of the sheep of the Lord is that they listen to His voice. Then there is only one shepherd and one flock.

Prayer: Lord, help me to view and see those that are meant to be in the same flock or family of God as I am. Help me to not be judgmental as people view things different than the way I do. Help me to be an aid to you in the strengthening and growth of your flock as you want it. Amen.

February 20

Mark 10:16 "Then he took the children in his arms and placed his hands on their heads and blessed them." NLT

In the short three year ministry term of Jesus it is clear that he made a careful note and attention for children.

We as his disciples and following ought to understand the value of children and their spirits and how we can coach them to become soldiers of Christ.

Jesus blessed the children and was very tender towards them - children are very important in all of our lives.

Prayer: Father I praise you for your love towards children. Help me to view them the way you do and to be attentive to them. Let me be used by you today to bring life them and encourage them in the ways of the Lord. Amen.

February 21

Titus 2:13 "Jesus Christ, who gave himself for us to redeem us from all wickedness and to purify for himself a people that are his very own, eager to do what is good." NIV

> The ultimate sacrifice - Jesus gave his entire life to us to redeem us. This makes us indebted to Him for eternity as our Savior.
>
> Redeeming us from all wickedness is not only past but also present and future. We are His people and wickedness should be far from us.
>
> Not only are we His people but we ought to be eager to do what is good. It should be a growing nature in us as we transform into His image and to want to do good.

Prayer: Father I thank you for your wonderful redemption. Never will I get tired of thanking you for saving my soul. I ask you Lord, to keep renewing my mind that I may grow in every way, to be like You and be far from wickedness. Amen.

February 22

Matthew 5:16 "In the same way, let your light shine before men, that they may see your good deeds and praise your Father in heaven." NIV

> We are a light to the world and everything we do should reflect Christ and draw people to the light.
>
> What we do should reflect who we are.
>
> Everything we do for others should be to the honor and praise of God. Our good deeds are a reflection of our love for the Lord.

Prayer: Lord I praise you for your goodness and that you are good all the time. Help me to reflect that goodness in everything I do and to everyone that they may honor and praise you too. Amen.

February 23

Luke 22:32 "But I have prayed for you, Simon, that your faith may not fail." NIV

Praise the name of the Lord - Jesus has prayed for us. In every situation He petitions for us.

His prayer is that our faith will not fail us - our faith is what is under violent attack. The devil doesn't care to destroy what we have but he is rather looking for an opportunity where he can make us think that God has forsaken us. That is what he is after!

That our faith wouldn't fail - no matter how violently we are attacked the Lord's prayer will undergird us. We must press through and trust the Lord. Without faith it is impossible to please Him.

Prayer: Lord I thank you for your faithfulness and that you have prayed for me. Help me Lord then, to diligently push through and not to give up. And to know that all these attacks are just the ploy of the enemy to diminish my faith. Strengthen my faith I pray in Jesus name. Amen.

February 24

Psalm 32:8 "I will instruct you and teach you in the way you should go; I will counsel you and watch over you." NIV

The Lord continually teaches us if we are willing to hear and listen.

He guides us where He wants us to walk in His perfect will - it takes deliberate submission and love for the Lord to want to go the way He has prepared for us.

He counsels us when we have questions and in the difficulties we face. We have the insurance that He watches over us. Hallelujah!

Prayer: Lord I praise you that you watch over me night and day and that I can depend upon your council when I face difficult situations. I praise and thank you Lord that you instruct and teach me and I submit willingly to you today. Amen.

February 25

1 Peter 5:8 "Be self-controlled and alert. Your enemy the devil prowls around like a roaring lion looking for someone to devour." NIV

The enemy (the devil) is a very real opposition to all of us and it takes being alert to the subtle tricks and problems he tries to distract us with.

Being self-controlled means to have discipline in our lives and not to be ruled by emotions or bad habits.

The devil is compared to a roaring lion and is constantly looking for something to devour. As a lion looks for the prey that is struggling or weak, so does the enemy and we have to avoid being an easy prey.

Prayer: Lord I thank you that you overcame the enemy and I have nothing to fear. Help me to stay focused on you and be alert and self-controlled that I might watch out for his attacks and diversions. Thank you for giving me authority over the enemy and I thank you for discernment today. Amen.

February 26

Philippians 4:8 "Finally, brothers, whatever is true, whatever is noble, whatever is right, whatever is pure, whatever is lovely, whatever is admirable—if anything is excellent or praiseworthy—think about such things." NIV

We are instructed in the Word to take every thought in our lives captive. (2 Corinthians 10:5)

There is a war in our minds through fear, anxiety and concerns and it is there that we have to win the battle - in our minds!

So we make a choice to think on things that are good and wholesome as the scripture says, rather than dwelling in our minds on all the negative. It is a question of directing all our thoughts on what is good.

Prayer: Lord I thank you for your love and kindness and that you watch over me today. Help me to direct my thoughts to all that is good and pure that I may be effective and produce much fruit for your kingdom's sake today. Amen.

February 27

James 1:6-7 "But when he asks, he must believe and not doubt, because he who doubts is like a wave of the sea, blown and tossed by the wind. That man should not think he will receive anything from the Lord;" NIV

> We can ask the Lord for anything but we must first believe, because God wants to do that for us, and then not doubt when we ask because the enemy likes to sow doubt in our minds in any way he can.
>
> Someone who doubts, according to the scripture, is unstable and we are told he will not receive anything.
>
> It is the enemy's target to put doubt in our minds when we ask so that we don't have real expectancy to receive.

Prayer: Father I do ask you for the things I need and I thank you that you remove all fear and doubt from my mind. You not only will do these things, but you want to do them when I ask because you are faithful. I praise you for your faithfulness. Amen!

February 28

Ephesians 2:10 "For we are God's workmanship, created in Christ Jesus to do good works, which God prepared in advance for us to do." NIV

> We are not only God's creation but we are made in His very DNA!
>
> We are to do good deeds and function in such a way that men can see and glorify our Father in heaven.
>
> God has prepared all these things that we ought to do before we were even born.

Prayer: Lord I thank you that you have always had a plan for my life and that you are full of grace and mercy. Help me to fulfill and do all the works you have planned and set before me before I was even born. Amen.

March 1

Romans 14:1 "Accept him whose faith is weak, without passing judgment on disputable matters." NIV

> We are clearly told over and over again by Jesus not to judge anyone else.
>
> And we are to be gracious to those that do not have the same insights or faith as we do.
>
> It is godly to avoid all unimportant controversial doctrines and matters and focus on the more important things of the kingdom of God.

Prayer: Lord I commit myself to you and ask for your grace not to have any judgement or opinions of others and to have grace for those that don't always understand or see things the way I do. Help me Lord, to have discernment when things are not important or worth fighting over. I pray for your nature to be created in me today. Amen.

March 2

2 Corinthians 1:20 "For no matter how many promises God has made, they are "Yes" in Christ. And so through him the "Amen" is spoken by us to the glory of God." NIV

> God is a promise keeper!
>
> In Christ our promises are strengthened because of the completed work at calvary. They are "Yes"!
>
> When we agree with the promises and say "Amen" (let it be so - we agree).

Prayer: Lord I thank you for your promises which are true and confirmed in Christ and strengthened by Him. I cling to your promises and thank you for them. Give me strength today to be focused on what you have promised rather on what I see. Amen.

March 3

Matthew 18:14 "In the same way your Father in heaven is not willing that any of these little ones should be lost." NIV

> Every human being on earth is of extreme value to the Creator.
>
> No matter how far they've wandered away from Him or have sinned it is still God's will that not one should be lost.
>
> As children of God it is our obligation to do all we can to help everyone and anyone that does not know the Lord to find Him while there is still time.

Prayer: Father thank you for the salvation that you've been kind enough to give me and my household. I pray that you use me and direct me by your spirit every day to be a witness to others that I may be instrumental in bringing the lost to your kingdom. Amen.

March 4

Proverbs 14:16 "He who fears the Lord has a secure fortress, and for his children it will be a refuge." NIV

> He who fears/regards/adheres to the Lord has a promise of God's protection.
>
> When we call out to the Lord, we can be assured of His help and protection in the worst of times and His blessings will continue.
>
> Even our children and descendants will be assured because we have put our faith, trust and regard into the Lord. It is a way of securing our children's futures.

Prayer: I praise you Lord that you are a strong fortress around me as I fear and regard you and love you with all of my heart. Thank you that you will be fortress and refuge for my children and their children. Amen.

March 5

Ezekiel 37:3-4 "He asked me, "Son of man, can these bones live?" I said, "Sovereign Lord, you alone know." Then he said to me, "Prophesy to these bones and say to them, 'Dry bones, hear the word of the Lord!' NIV

> In our lives often we don't see the potential in what seems to be dead and gone (dry bones).
>
> In obedience to the Lord we need to speak life into it.
>
> When we speak and view what seems to have lost potential, in obedience to God, new life will come into it once again and miracles happen!

Prayer: Father, I praise you for you are great and are able to make even what seems to have passed and dead come back to life. Help me to see things the way you see them and to obey you when you speak and tell me to prophesy to my dead bones. Amen.

March 6

James 3:18 "Peacemakers who sow in peace reap a harvest of righteousness." NIV

The peacemakers are not the peacekeepers, which means that sometimes we need to make war to make peace.

But those that are peacemakers are promised a reward and harvest of righteousness and right standing with God. For He is our peace.

It is a lifestyle of pursuing God's peace which is nothing like the world's peace.

Prayer: Father, you are the God of peace and I thank you for the peace you give me, not as the world gives, but from heaven above. Help me to walk in your peace and to be a real peacemaker for your name's sake. Amen.

March 7

James 5:19-20 "My brothers and sisters, if one of you should wander from the truth and someone should bring that person back, remember this: Whoever turns a sinner from the error of their way will save them from death and cover over a multitude of sins." NIV

It is very possible, even being fully saved, to "wander" from the truth. We ought to be watchful of this both for ourselves and for those that we are responsible for around us.

There is a 'coming back' and we ought to be mindful to help those around us to be able to come back. It is our responsibility.

There is death that waits for those that wander off and we save them from that when we make an effort to help our brethren that have gotten cold. And in doing so we cover a whole multitude of sins!

Prayer: Lord I praise you for your amazing salvation. Keep me and my household true Lord. Help me to be an instrument to bring those that have wandered off back to their first love and the full light of the truth. Amen.

March 8

Colossians 3:10 "and have put on the new self, which is being renewed in knowledge in the image of its Creator." NIV

> We are born again - we have become a new creation. Old things have passed away and we are being renewed in our minds daily.
>
> We have to have ourselves renewed in knowledge, as knowledge changes our minds so that we may become what we actually were born again to become.
>
> There is a "putting off of the old self" - it takes a real effort to change behavioral patterns conforming to what the Lord has saved us to be.

Prayer: Thank you for saving my soul Lord and making me a new creation. Help me to take off the old and put on the new self daily, that I may take on your image and reflect you in every part of my life. Amen.

March 9

Matthew 16:27 "For the Son of Man is going to come in his Father's glory with his angels, and then he will reward each person according to what they have done." NIV

> The return of Christ is imminent - this is the one thing that all christians can agree on and expect!
>
> The return of Christ is not only triumphant but brings with it a brand new era with salvation.
>
> According to what we have done or admitted to do, we will be rewarded accordingly. There is a reward that He brings.

Prayer: Lord I look with excitement to your second coming and return. In my heart I am excited for that day. Help me to be ever busy with that reward in mind that I may be pleasing in your sight, both now and then. Amen.

March 10

John 16:33 "I have told you these things, so that in me you may have peace. In this world you will have trouble. But take heart! I have overcome the world." NIV

> It is the desire of the Lord for us to have peace in Him. There is no other place, or way to seek peace, other than in the Lord.
>
> It would be no surprise to any of us, with these words of Jesus, that we will have and expect trouble in this world.
>
> The reassurance with all our trouble is the He overcame the world and is able to secure us. We have nothing to fear.

Prayer: Lord I thank you for your peace which surpasses all understanding. And I pray that you give me courage to face all troubles that are in this world, knowing that you have overcome it. Amen.

March 11

Psalm 65:4 "Blessed are those you choose and bring near to live in your courts! We are filled with the good things of your house, of your holy temple." NIV

As many are called, few are chosen. It is a privilege to be called of the Lord and even more so to be chosen. Jesus said we did not choose Him, He chose us.

We get to live in the courts, in a relationship and closeness with the Lord - all because of the work of Jesus at calvary.

Blessings of every nature come with being in His presence and in relationship with Him.

Prayer: Lord I thank you that you called me and chose me. My heart is overwhelmed to know that my name is in the Lamb's book of life and that you love me. Thank you for all the good things I enjoy in my relationship with you. Amen.

March 12

Ephesians 1:3 "Praise be to the God and Father of our Lord Jesus Christ, who has blessed us in the heavenly realms with every spiritual blessing in Christ." NIV

> We have so much blessings that are from heaven above and we ought to be grateful for all His blessings.
>
> All the blessings that we receive are through Christ and because of Christ. Not one blessing are we deserving of, nor should we expect it for any other reason than the completed work of Jesus.
>
> We ought to name our blessings continually, giving thanks for them.

Prayer: Father, I thank you for the completed work of Christ and all the blessings that we have in Him and through Him that are from heaven above. I am truly a blessed person today and praise your wonderful name for it. You are worthy of all praise. Amen.

March 13

1 Peter 2:9 "But you are a chosen people, a royal priesthood, a holy nation, God's special possession, that you may declare the praises of him who called you out of darkness into his wonderful light." NIV

> He chose us - We didn't choose Him and we ought to be thrilled and full of joy because He chose us.
>
> We actually "belong" to God so we ought to declare His praises continually.
>
> When He called us, He called us from darkness into the light - He is the Lord of light!

Prayer: Father I thank you that you chose me and that I am called out of darkness in to the light. Help me to continually walk in the light as you are light. I surrender my life to you with gladness, knowing you have redeemed me and I thank you for it. Help me to share this wonderful light today with someone. Amen.

March 14

Colossians 3:17 "And whatever you do, whether in word or deed, do it all in the name of the Lord Jesus, giving thanks to God the Father through him." NIV

> No matter what we do - that means anything and everything - it must be done for the Lord as onto the Lord; not for man that we expect an award or thanks from them.
>
> Giving thanks to the Lord - thankfulness should be a complete and ongoing developing of life. The Lord loves a thankful heart and also dislikes an unthankful heart.
>
> We have so much life "through" Jesus. He is our savior, our shield, our Lord and our high mediator.

Prayer: Lord I dedicate this day, and my life, to you with everything I do is for you as if I am doing for you. My expectancy is in you that you will reward me, bless me and look after me. Amen.

March 15

Hebrews 13:8 "Jesus Christ is the same yesterday and today and forever." NIV

God absolutely never changes! Regardless of our changing circumstances and situations, we can always rely that He is consistently unchanging.

Life offers so many changing situations and challenges every day. Often we are taken by surprise of things unexpected.

We should always revert back to this knowledge and not assume that God has changed His attitude or opinion towards us because of some situation we are facing. He never changes!

Prayer: Lord I thank you that you are unchanging and that I can always depend on your faithfulness and consistent love that never fails. Thank you for the favor upon my life. Help me today to not look at my circumstances or situations but to be confident in your greatness and unchanging faithfulness. Amen.

March 16

Hebrews 2:16 "For surely it is not angels he helps, but Abraham's descendants." NIV

> Though Angels are powerful they were not made in the image of God.
>
> He is focused on us - He sent His only son for us alone!
>
> We are more important and more valuable than angels.

Prayer: Father I thank you for making me in your image and that I have your DNA. Help me to walk as your child and to keep pursuing you in relationship. I need you and cannot live without you. Fill me with your presence and your love today. Amen.

March 17

Genesis 3:9 "But the Lord God called to the man, "Where are you?"" NIV

It was in the cool of the day that God was looking for Adam and Eve. A certain sliver of time in the full 24 hours of their lives that God wanted to interact with them.

He wants to interact with us, even if just for a short time every day.

Is He looking for you too? He looked for Adam because he was not where he was supposed to be in their meeting place. Let us be sure to be where the Lord can find us.

Prayer: Lord I do want to meet you and fellowship with you. You are the most important thing in my life. Help me to be diligent and faithful to meet with you every day. I love you Lord and commit my life to you. Amen.

March 18

1 Corinthians 12:31 "Now eagerly desire the greater gifts. And yet I will show you the most excellent way." NIV

> We are to desire to be functioning in different giftings and to be effective.
>
> There is a more excellent way - It is the way that surpasses all the giftings and all the effectiveness of all the abilities - Love.
>
> We ask to desire the greater gifts but there is something even greater than that. We ought to pursue His love.

Prayer: Lord you are love and I pray that you fill me with yourself and your love that I may share that love with everyone I meet today. Amen.

March 19

Romans 8:3 "For what the law was powerless to do because it was weakened by the flesh, God did by sending his own Son in the likeness of sinful flesh to be a sin offering. And so he condemned sin in the flesh," NIV

> The law and trying to do what is right in man's efforts had no power and no effect.
>
> The completed work of Christ dying on the cross satisfied that penalty that we needed to pay.
>
> Jesus came in the "likeness" of a sinful man to be our savior and offering for all our sin.

Prayer: Father I thank you that you have sent Jesus to die for me and that though He condemned the sin He shows grace and mercy to the sinner. Help me to have that attitude to all those around me and to understand this in my own heart - that you have forgiven me and redeemed me. Help me to be gracious to all those I meet today. Amen.

March 20

Galatians 5:6 "For in Christ Jesus neither circumcision nor uncircumcision has any value. The only thing that counts is faith expressing itself through love." NIV

> The dead works that symbolize nothing without Christ.
>
> The only thing that counts is faith ...
>
> To express faith without love is dead.
> Love and faith shake hands and is encompassed by grace.

Prayer: Lord fill me with your love and help me to walk in faith. Help me to express it daily. Rather than pursuing dead works, help me to be a doer of your word by walking in faith. I confess and admit that I cannot do this without you. Be my strength today. Amen.

March 21

Hebrews 6:12 "We do not want you to become lazy, but to imitate those who through faith and patience inherit what has been promised." NIV

> We are not to be become tired or lazy or weary in our doing.
>
> We should follow the example of those who, through faith and patience, endured until they achieved what they believed for.
>
> There is definitely a time when we are awarded for being patient and keeping our confidence and faith in God - sometimes we are stretched to the max but He will never test us above what we are able.

Prayer: Lord I thank you that you give me the grace to not get lazy or weary but to imitate those that have set an example of enduring by faith to inherit the promise that you gave them. Help me then, to not give up but continue to press in and believe in you because you are faithful. Amen.

March 22

Joshua 24:15 "But as for me and my household, we will serve the Lord." NIV

Serving God, ourselves and our household, is a clear choice that we make.

Sometimes we are alone in that choice as many around us, who are important to us, find it undesirable.

It is a price we pay when we choose to serve God but the end result and rewards are uncountable.

Prayer: Lord help me to always be the one to choose to serve you and impart to my household to put you first and serve you with all our hearts. Amen.

March 23

Ephesians 5:17 "Therefore do not be foolish, but understand what the Lord's will is." NIV

God didn't save us with the expensive price of His own son's blood only to have us struggling to know His will.

It is easier to know God's will than we think. We are born again and are one with Him and it just takes practice to become quiet before Him to hear what He says.

It takes real effort to miss God and make a mistake because He keeps us, through nudging and confirmation in different situations, on the path He wants us to walk.

Prayer: Lord I thank you for saving me with the great price you paid. I pray that you continue to lead me and help me to hear clearly what your will is for my life, and to fulfill that will with excitement. Amen.

March 24

John 6:35 "I am the bread of life. Whoever comes to me will never go hungry, and whoever believes in me will never be thirsty." NIV

> The Lord is all we have or will ever need.
>
> He satisfies us with so many good things in so many ways, but it takes growth and dedication to the Lord to learn to be satisfied with what He gives and not always want something else.
>
> It is a promise of God that we will not be lacking for anything - not hungry or thirsty for anything, both naturally and spiritually - He satisfies. It is a promise we can rely on!

Prayer: Lord I thank you for your wonderful love and kindness towards me, my family and all your children. I pray that you always help my attitude to be one of gratitude and joy for that which you give to sustain me. All my hunger and all my thirst! Amen.

March 25

Mark 9:39 39 "Do not stop him," Jesus said. "No one who does a miracle in my name can in the next moment say anything bad about me 40 for whoever is not against us is for us. NIV

The family of God is much bigger than just the people we know.

It is counter productive to the Kingdom to criticize other doctrines or Christians, God never appointed any one to be policemen in His Kingdom. He will build His Kingdom.

Jesus told Peter to focus on following Him rather than trying to assess others and their walk with Him. (John 21:20-22)

Prayer: Father I love You and thank You for saving me. Help me to see all Your children through Your eyes and maintain my focus on what You have given me to do today. Amen.

March 26

Acts 23:1 'And looking intently at the council, Paul said, "Brothers, I have lived my life before God in all good conscience up to this day."' ESV

> We only have one life to live - there are no do overs and each day should be carefully lived before the Lord.
>
> Living our life before God helps influence our decision.
>
> Good conscience - often God will use our conscience to help guide us, so that we will have the right motives and a clear conscience before God in all we do.

Prayer: Lord I pray that you help me to continue to walk with you and before you with a clear conscience. Help me to live every day accountable to you only. I give my life and my time to you. Amen.

March 27

Ephesians 3:16 "I pray that out of his glorious riches he may strengthen you with power through his Spirit in your inner being," NIV

God has an abundant supply - glorious riches - And He will give according to whatever we need or ask for.

He will strengthen us with His power because when we are weak He is strong in our weakness.

Our inner man needs strengthening to endure and to exemplify Christ in every given situation.

Prayer: Lord I thank you that your anointing and your power strengthens me in my inner man so that I can be a testimony and a reflection of your greatness. I am nothing without you and depend completely on you. Amen.

March 28

Matthew 11:29 "Take my yoke upon you and learn from me, for I am gentle and humble in heart, and you will find rest for your souls." NIV

> Putting His yoke upon us - His yoke is light and is not burdensome. When we are overburdened, it did not come from Him.
>
> Be gentle and humble of heart and follow His example - there we will find rest.
>
> Learning from Him is a working process and an ongoing experience.

Prayer: Lord I thank you, as I take your yoke upon myself, that is not only easy and light but it brings me rest in my soul. I gladly submit myself to you and follow your ways completely with confidence and faith in you. Amen.

March 29

1 John 2:15 "Do not love the world or anything in the world. If anyone loves the world, love for the Father is not in them." NIV

Our love should be for the Lord first and foremost - we are told explicitly not to love this world.

We cannot love both the world and God, one of them will be neglected. We have to choose who is going to be first.

God will never let us down. So if we choose to love Him with all of our hearts, we'll only be blessed and fulfilled in our hearts and lives.

Prayer: Lord, I choose you as Lord and Savior in every way, shape and form. Lead me in your ways and help me to continually love you with all of my heart and not the world. To be in this world but not of this world. Thank you for your strength today. Amen.

March 30

Psalms 119:133 "Direct my footsteps according to your word; let no sin rule over me." NIV

> The Lord will guide us in the way He wants us to go if we are willing to follow.
>
> His word is a lamp to our feet and a guide for our lives and we ought to live by His word.
>
> We ought not to be slaves to sin or have sin rule over our lives. We should be totally His.

Prayer: Lord I thank you that you direct my footsteps daily and that you have set me free from sin. I give you this day and my heart once again and ask you to rule every area of my life. Amen.

March 31

Luke 24:46-47 "He told them, "This is what is written: The Messiah will suffer and rise from the dead on the third day, and repentance for the forgiveness of sins will be preached in his name to all nations" NIV

> A completed work on calvary - not just death - but resurrection also.
>
> The redemption now being complete, the doors for salvation are open. Jesus said;"the forgiveness of sins will be preached" and it is our job to further this message because of what we have received and what Christ has done.
>
> We do not dwell in only half of things being fulfilled in our own lives, such as death, but also the resurrection. There might be a momentary sadness but it will be a longtime rejoicing.

Prayer: Father today I do not only rejoice that you have died for us, but rose from the grave for us that we can also be resurrected and enjoy eternity with you. Thank you for this complete and amazing salvation. Amen.

April 1

1 Peter 2:21 "For God called you to do good, even if it means suffering, just as Christ suffered for you. He is your example, and you must follow in his steps" NLT

> We were made, saved and redeemed to do good - only good!
>
> Doing good isn't always pleasant or the easiest thing to do but it is certainly God's way.
>
> Suffering is usually an indication of the dead old self. The more we abandon ourselves to Christ, the less painful and uncomfortable the things we do for the Lord become.

Prayer: Lord I lay my life on the altar as a living sacrifice to you today. I choose to do good even if it is uncomfortable or causes me difficulty. Give me the grace to do these things. Amen.

April 2

Ephesians 5:2 "Live a life filled with love, following the example of Christ. He loved us and offered himself as a sacrifice for us, a pleasing aroma to God." NLT

A life of love - means adopting and entire life style. We are unable to do this in our own strength. We need complete dedication to Him that He can fill us with Himself; He Himself being love.

Christ is our example of what love really looks like; unselfish, self-sacrificing, and obedient to the max.

It pleases the Lord when we function in love. And love is not to be confused with human "liking". We have a clear definition of love in 1 Corinthians 13.

Prayer: Lord, fill me with your love today. I desire to be a vessel of your love to all. Not just the ones I like but all those you send my way. Help me to even love the unlovable. Amen.

April 3

John 6:63 "The Spirit alone gives eternal life. Human effort accomplishes nothing. And the very words I have spoken to you are spirit and life." NLT

> We are spirit beings and eternity awaits us away from this body.
>
> Our human efforts do not achieve very much and we spend way too much time on the human side of our lives instead of the spiritual.
>
> We depend upon the very words of life that come from our Lord - Heaven and earth was created by words alone.

Prayer: Lord help me to focus on your word and what you say to me. Let your word live inside of me that I may produce more life in the spirit than the things of the flesh. Amen.

April 4

Psalms 63:7 "Because you are my helper, I sing for joy in the shadow of your wings. I cling to you; your strong right hand holds me securely." NLT

> We wouldn't need to call upon the Lord as our helper if we didn't have challenges. Challenges are part of our life's journey.
>
> We ought to sing and constantly keep our joy focused on the source of our joy - Him.
>
> We need to know that we are secure in His right hand, regardless of our circumstances and situation.

Prayer: Lord I sing your joy today and praise you because I am safe in your arms regardless my situation. I thank you that you are my helper and my source. Amen.

April 5

Proverbs 3:24 "When you lie down, you will not be afraid; when you lie down, your sleep will be sweet." NIV

> We spend an entire third of our lives sleeping - sleeping is a very important part of our well being.
>
> So many of us have disturbed and restless sleep but it is God's plan for us to have peaceful, pleasant sleep.
>
> We never ought to allow our sleep stolen by the enemy or situations and circumstances for He is our peace.

Prayer: Lord I thank you for restful sleep and for the peace you give more than the world can give. I claim my sleep at night to be full of rest and peace. I praise you for it! Amen.

April 6

Matthew 20:28 " just as the Son of Man did not come to be served, but to serve, and to give his life as a ransom for many." NIV

The epitome and image of Christianity is all about serving and not wanting to be served or to receive. A totality of giving of one self.

Jesus, who is the example and Lord of all, set the bar and example by serving in every way.

Jesus laid down His life as a ransom - if we love our lives, we will lose it. We ought to surrender our lives into His hands.

Prayer: Lord I give my life to you today and look for opportunities to serve others and lay down my life. Help me to be alert of these opportunities so I may find joy in serving you today. Amen.

April 7

Romans 11:36 "For from him and through him and for him are all things. To him be the glory forever! Amen." NIV

We have to be reminded frequently who the center of the universe and our existence is - the Lord God alone!

Everything is through Him and from Him and nothing is separate from Him. In all our circumstances we need to acknowledge and realize that God is bigger than any situation.

It is easy to be influenced by people and our fears and forget that He is the center of it all.

Prayer: Lord I acknowledge you as sovereign and God. I know that all things come through you, to you and because of you. Help me to be reminded daily that you are my God and in control. I praise you that my life is in your hands. Amen.

April 8

Habakkuk 3:17-18 "Though the fig tree does not bud and there are no grapes on the vines, though the olive crop fails and the fields produce no food, though there are no sheep in the pen and no cattle in the stalls, yet I will rejoice in the Lord, I will be joyful in God my Savior." NIV

There are various seasons in our lives; winters are unavoidable even though we all crave for the spring and summers.

Sometimes it seems that all is hopeless and lost in the season we find ourselves in but take courage that God is still God!

Yet - I will rejoice - we will always be content in the Lord because He is the source of it all. And by His grace we will be happy in the Lord and not be swayed by our circumstances.

Prayer: Father I thank you for always being my helper and provider. And even though my circumstances seem bleak and hopeless, I rejoice because you are unchanged and the source of it all. I praise you and thank you that you will take care of me. Amen.

April 9

1 Peter 3:8 "Finally, all of you, be like-minded, be sympathetic, love one another, be compassionate and humble." NIV

Living in harmony takes real effort as some people are difficult, as we are, in getting along with in relationships.

The Lord gives us grace and fills us with His love to love others and to be sympathetic and compassionate.

Being humble is a lifetime endeavor - the beginning of which starts with genuine thankfulness.

Prayer: Lord it is my heart's desire to do all that is right and pleasing in your sight. I pray that you fill me with your love and compassion for others that I not only live in harmony, but be a blessing to other people today. Amen.

April 10

Matthew 7:26 "But anyone who hears my teaching and doesn't obey it is foolish, like a person who builds a house on sand." NLT

>Once we hear His word/ teaching we become responsible to act on it.

>It is foolishness if we do not apply His way and what He teaches. It is so fruitful and effective for our lives.

>It creates a solid foundation for everything we do if we put into action what He teaches.

Prayer: Lord help me to hear clearly what you teach and help me also to put it into effect on a daily basis. Remind me of your ways that I may grow and build my house upon the rock. Amen.

April 11

Romans 8:8 "That's why those who are still under the control of their sinful nature can never please God." NLT

>We are not to be controlled by our old sinful nature - we need the Holy Spirit to help us master that.
>
>The sinful nature and its desires only lead to death and rebel against God and we want to be in obedience and listen to Him.
>
>The end product of a sinful nature and its decisions and motivations only brings destruction even in the natural and there is no life in it - God's ways are always a 100% better.

Prayer: Lord I pray that you help me overcome my sinful nature and help me to walk by your spirit and your ways all the days of my life. I confess that I am weak and I need your strength because when I am weak you are strong. Amen.

April 12

1 Timothy 1:16 "But God had mercy on me so that Christ Jesus could use me as a prime example of his great patience with even the worst sinners. Then others will realize that they, too, can believe in him and receive eternal life." NLT

> God's great mercy - there is just no expressing in words this great mercy He bestows on us. Even after we're saved.
>
> We ought to be examples to others in our lives and not be boastful thinking we are any better. As God has shown mercy to us we should show mercy to others.
>
> We are all redeemed and the redeemed of the Lord should say so! We are redeemed by His mercy

Prayer: Father help me to be a living example to others on a continual basis. Let them see that I have been redeemed and what great work you have done in my life. Amen.

April 13

Matthew 6:31-32 "So don't worry about these things, saying, 'What will we eat? What will we drink? What will we wear?' These things dominate the thoughts of unbelievers, but your heavenly Father already knows all your needs." NLT

> Jesus taught us not to worry about our every day life needs - not to worry or concern ourselves.
>
> These things dominate the thoughts of unbelievers - if you are an unbeliever and not trusting the Lord these concerns dominate your thought life and it becomes the most important thing to you.
>
> Our Father already knows everything we need before we ask. He has it all taken care of.

Prayer: Father help me today to not be concerned about my daily needs or things that I feel I am lacking, but rather be full of joy knowing that you are already aware of all my needs and will supply all that I need. Amen.

April 14

James 4:14 "How do you know what your life will be like tomorrow? Your life is like the morning fog—it's here a little while, then it's gone." NLT

We are called to live for today as His name is "I am" and the Lord wants us to only concern ourselves with the now.

We do not know what our life is tomorrow. We make so many plans for our future but we have no guarantees or understanding what tomorrow holds. It is all in His hands.

Life is like the morning fog - it goes by so quickly and we should not be overly concerned or frantic about tomorrow or that which has less importance.

Prayer: I praise you Lord for saving me and that my eternal life is secure in you as I follow you today. Give me the grace to not be concerned about my future or try to make plans for tomorrow that are of less importance but to be focused on your leading. Amen.

April 15

Ephesians 5:20 "And give thanks for everything to God the Father in the name of our Lord Jesus Christ." NLT

Giving thanks for everything means in everything we go through we give thanks because we know that God is in control and sovereign.

When we develop a thankful spirit and a heart of gratitude in our daily lives, we not only have full joy but also gain a humble attitude before the Lord.

It is all because of our Lord that we give thanks and we should always acknowledge Him.

Prayer: Lord I praise you and give you thanks for all that you have done and are doing. I give you the glory and praise in every circumstance and in your name because there is no other name given where by which man shall be saved. I thank you for your love and kindness today and that you will lead me. My heart rejoices for all that you are and all that you are doing. Amen.

April 16

Romans 5:5 "And this hope will not lead to disappointment. For we know how dearly God loves us, because he has given us the Holy Spirit to fill our hearts with his love." NLT

> Hope - positive expectancy - the Lord will never lead us into any kind of disappointment. Our expectancy in HIM is always safe.
>
> God loves us so intensely that He has given us the Holy Spirit to fill us so we can taste of how much He loves us.
>
> Only the Holy Spirit can fill our hearts with His love.

Prayer: Lord I thank you for this hope of salvation and trust in you that will never disappointment me. Thank you for your amazing love that fills my heart. Help me to fully embrace that love today. Amen.

April 17

Matthew 18:3 "And he said: "Truly I tell you, unless you change and become like little children, you will never enter the kingdom of heaven." NIV

It is clear that we are not automatically like little children and it takes effort to change.

The essence of the attitude of a child is so trusting and open.

We cannot even enter into the supernatural or heavenly realms of understanding unless we have this mind change with the act of humility and simplicity of a child.

Prayer: Lord I purpose in my heart today to humble my heart and become like a child that I may not only enter the Kingdom, but also grow and become fruitful for Your Kingdom sake. Amen.

April 18

Ephesians 4:29 "Do not let any unwholesome talk come out of your mouths, but only what is helpful for building others up according to their needs, that it may benefit those who listen." NIV

> We need to control what comes out of our mouths - unwholesome talk would be described as anything that is lifeless and unpleasant.
>
> What comes out of our mouths should be beneficial to others and to help make them strong in the Lord.
>
> The things that come our of mouths should be of good effect and help to all those listening -in other words, fruitful words.

Prayer: Lord I pray that your anointing will reside in my mind and on my tongue today so that I will only speak words that are life-giving and fruitful. Help me to curb all idle words and things that are not wholesome. Amen.

April 19

John 10:14-15 "I am the good shepherd; I know my own sheep, and they know me, just as my Father knows me and I know the Father. So I sacrifice my life for the sheep." NLT

> There is a "knowing" between the shepherd and the sheep - when you are in a relationship with Him He knows us and we know Him.
>
> There is no one that compares to Jesus and His shepherding and commitment - He gave the ultimate sacrifice for us.
>
> In comparison our relationship with Him is compared to the relationship He has with the Father. The Unity.

Prayer: Father I thank you for Jesus and His sacrifice. Thank you Lord that you are the good shepherd and I am so grateful that you are my shepherd. Help me to have that commitment not only to You, but to my brethren also. Help me to imitate and reflect Your goodness toward me and everything I do for others. Amen.

April 20

1 Timothy 1:16 "But for that very reason I was shown mercy so that in me, the worst of sinners, Christ Jesus might display his immense patience as an example for those who would believe in him and receive eternal life." NIV

> We have received amazing mercy and grace from Him that forgives us daily. Praise Him!

> The worst of sinners - no limit to what the worst of sinners could have done, there is forgiveness and complete restoration. He is full of kindness and mercy.

> Unlimited patience is only possible in Him. We, in our humanity, often get impatient but the Lord has no limit to His patience.

Prayer: Lord I thank you for this amazing salvation and as I grow to know You and Your unlimited kindness, mercy and patience, create in me that heart that You have that I may display Your love every day. Amen.

April 21

Isaiah 26:3 "You will keep in perfect peace those whose minds are steadfast, because they trust in you." NIV

> There is no peace that compares to the peace that the Lord gives.
>
> Life has so many challenges and turmoil and we can be grateful for the joy and peace that comes from the Lord, even while we are in the turmoil.
>
> We have to focus our minds on Him and His Word. All thoughts need to be taken captive and directed on Him.

Prayer: Lord I ask you today to take my mind and all my thoughts captive that I may focus on you only. Help me to walk in your perfect peace, day and night, no matter what troubles I go through. I praise you for it. In Jesus name. Amen.

April 22

John 15:16 "You did not choose me, but I chose you and appointed you so that you might go and bear fruit—fruit that will last—and so that whatever you ask in my name the Father will give you." NIV

> Often we think we chose the Lord but He chose us!
>
> It was always God's plan that we are fruitful and display all that the Lord has done in us through our lives.
>
> When we start to function and be fruitful the Father will give us anything we ask.

Prayer: Thank you for choosing me Lord. Help me to be fruitful today and to be all that you have designed me to be. Amen.

April 23

Romans 10:13 "Everyone who calls on the name of the Lord will be saved." NIV

> It is the plan and the desire of the Lord that each one on the face of the earth be born again, saved - not one to be lost.
>
> To get someone to call on the Lord with a sincere heart, is the target.
>
> It is an amazing gospel - all those who "call" will be saved.

Prayer: Father help me to be conscious daily of reaching out to those who do not know you, to help them call on you so they may be saved. Amen.

April 24

Matthew 7:24 "Therefore everyone who hears these words of mine and puts them into practice is like a wise man who built his house on the rock." NIV

> Hearing His word is more than just listening. It is actually receiving with an open heart and understanding.
>
> Then hearing is not enough - we have to put it into practice and do that word for it to actually have an effect.
>
> His word is life changing and security when we do what He says.

Prayer: Lord I thank you for Your words. Help me to hear them deep in my heart and to do exactly what You say. I praise You for how great You are! Amen.

April 25

1 John 5:4 "for everyone born of God overcomes the world. This is the victory that has overcome the world, even our faith." NIV

> It is God's design that we overcome and be over-comers.
>
> It is our faith in the Lord and His word that gives us the victory and the power to overcome.
>
> To have faith and to operate in faith we have to be born of God.

Prayer: Lord I thank you for your salvation and that I am born of you. Thank you that my faith is growing daily by hearing your word, that I may overcome the world and be an overcomer today. Amen.

April 26

2 Corinthians 7:1 "Therefore, since we have these promises, dear friends, let us purify ourselves from everything that contaminates body and spirit, perfecting holiness out of reverence for God." NIV

> Purifying ourselves or being sanctified is a continual process of relationship with Him.
>
> Perfecting holiness is walking in His presence continually and being enveloped in Him.
>
> The reason we do it is because we love Him and He is the center of our hearts and world.

Prayer: Lord I thank you for your promises and by your grace I desire to walk in sanctification on a daily basis and purify my heart. I pray that you give me grace to grow and change to become more like you Lord. Amen.

April 27

Genesis 16:13 "She gave this name to the Lord who spoke to her: "You are the God who sees me," for she said, "I have now seen the One who sees me." NIV

> The Lord is mindful of us and watches over us.
>
> We do not have to list our plights or difficulties because the Lord is watching and very much aware of each of us.
>
> His grace and mercy and love for us is limitless.

Prayer: Lord I thank you that You do see me and watch over me regardless of what I see or feel today. I take rest in Your awareness and love for me. Amen.

April 28

Hebrews 6:17 "Because God wanted to make the unchanging nature of his purpose very clear to the heirs of what was promised, he confirmed it with an oath." NIV

> God's purpose for us - each individually - does not change!
>
> We are heirs of His promise; that means we will inherit from Him exactly what He promises.
>
> He confirms it with a promise or an oath - God's word is always "yes and amen".

Prayer: Lord I thank you for your purpose in my life and that you have called me. Help me to walk in obedience and fulfill the destiny you have planned for me and not to be distracted by "bumps" in the road. Amen.

April 29

2 Timothy 1:12 "Yet this is no cause for shame, because I know whom I have believed, and am convinced that he is able to guard what I have entrusted to him until that day." NIV

> We are not to be ashamed when we are standing for the Lord but to be bold.
>
> It is through relationship that we know Him and believe in Him.
>
> He will watch over His word and guard what we give to Him to be sovereign over - we trust and entrust our lives to Him.

Prayer: Lord I praise you for your goodness and that I am able to entrust my life, my family and my future into your hands. I praise you today knowing you have everything under control. Amen.

April 30

Philippians 3:8 "What is more, I consider everything a loss because of the surpassing worth of knowing Christ Jesus my Lord, for whose sake I have lost all things. I consider them garbage, that I may gain Christ." NIV

Many of the things we chase after in this world, even if we get them, seem to be empty and have no life to them.

Jesus is the complete joy and fulfillment of everything in our lives and worth so much more than what we valued before.

We may have to surrender some of the things we thought we valued to gain the greater treasure of knowing Him and enjoying Him.

Prayer: Lord I lay everything down at the altar today, everything I have and everything I've done, and I choose you. You are the first and most important desire of my heart. My heart is yours Lord and I praise you that you lead me where you want me to go. Amen.

May 1

Romans 13:1 "Let everyone be subject to the governing authorities, for there is no authority except that which God has established. The authorities that exist have been established by God." NIV

> Not all authorities or those in authority are agreeable to our understanding or seem godly.
>
> It is the will of God and the way of the Lord that we show ourselves exemplary in submission to those in authority over us.
>
> We cannot exercise authority if we do not recognize authority.

Prayer: Lord I thank you that I can be assured in my heart that all authority is established by you. Help me to be submissive in my heart and not be critical with my mouth towards those you have put in authority. Help me to be christ-like to those you have given me authority over so I may be an example in every way. Amen.

May 2

John 14:27 "Peace I leave with you; my peace I give you. I do not give to you as the world gives. Do not let your hearts be troubled and do not be afraid." NIV

> Fear is the mirror image of faith and does not come from God but rather from the enemy.
>
> Fear and troubled hearts steal and hinder our peace which is our birthright and gift from God which He dearly paid for.
>
> We ought to avoid our hearts being troubled and when we have to face these things we pray until we maintain the peace He has promised us.

Prayer: Lord I thank you for this peace that the world cannot give. Help me to continue to walk in your peace today and for the rest of my life. I pray that your Holy Spirit will guard me against a troubled heart and fear. Amen.

May 3

John 3:8 The wind blows wherever it pleases. You hear its sound, but you cannot tell where it comes from or where it is going. So it is with everyone born of the Spirit. NIV

> Even though the Holy Spirit seems mysterious, evidence of the Holy Spirit is visible and gloriously effective.
>
> The Holy Spirit may seem mysterious to those unfamiliar with Him, but we love and embrace Him.
>
> We are spirit beings living in a body and, so then, born of the Spirit.

Prayer: Father. I thank You for the Holy Spirit and that You have sent Him to be our comforter and to lead us. Help me today to be sensitive to Him.

May 4

Psalm 29:11 "The Lord gives strength to his people; the Lord blesses his people with peace." NIV

>We are His people, called by His name, redeemed by His blood.

>He gives us strength which we so often need in different situations.

>It is a blessing to receive His peace.

Prayer: Father, how I praise you today that I am yours and that you strengthen me that I may walk in your peace and grace today. Bless me this day that I can be a blessing to others. Amen.

May 5

James 3:18 "Peacemakers who sow in peace reap a harvest of righteousness." NIV

> Peace makers are not peace keepers - keeping the peace is pacifying people.
>
> Sometimes we have to make a little "war" to make the peace.
>
> We have to love God's peace and His way to actually be a peace maker - then to reap that reward.

Prayer: Lord I praise you that you are Lord and I ask that you grant me grace to be a genuine peace maker, not to please the people but to please you, and to bring peace between my neighbors. Give me wisdom today I pray in Jesus name. Amen.

May 6

Galatians 5:24-25 "Those who belong to Christ Jesus have crucified the flesh with its passions and desires. Since we live by the Spirit, let us keep in step with the Spirit." NIV

> When we belong to the Lord we put away old behavior and sinful desires. If we see evidence of these things we need to gravitate more towards Him in our relationship.
>
> Living by the Spirit means to, not only strengthen our relationship with Him, but to be mindful of Him every waking moment.
>
> Keeping in stead with the Spirit means to take our cues and leading from Him.

Prayer: Lord I ask you to help me today to make sure that my fleshly desires and passions are crucified daily that I can follow after you and to walk in the Spirit. Help me Holy Spirit to be sensitive and adhere to you each day and the rest of my life. Amen.

May 7

Psalms 139:23 "Search me, God, and know my heart; test me and know my anxious thoughts." NIV

We should always remember that God can examine our hearts to check our motives.

Our hearts, that belong to Him, should always be willing to be searched and examined to keep maintaining the right heart attitude and motives.

Jesus told us not to be anxious for anything and we ought not to have anxious thoughts.

Prayer: Lord, I give you permission to search my heart and motives and to see that I walk in faith and uprightness before you. Amen.

May 8

2 Peter 3:18 "But grow in the grace and knowledge of our Lord and Savior Jesus Christ." NIV

Once we're saved we have to maintain consistent growth. Standing still is not an option as it really equates to going backwards.

Grace - the undeserved favor and knowledge of our Lord Jesus is what we grow in, a continual basis to work from.

The way we grow in this is to maintain a relationship with Him by talking and communing with Him every day through reading His Word and making time for our Lord.

Prayer: Father I ask you to help me grow today in the knowledge and grace of our Lord Jesus. Help me Father to always protect my intimacy with you. I pray that you will strengthen me today that I can grow and bear much fruit. Amen.

May 9

Philippians 1:21 "For to me, to live is Christ and to die is gain." NIV

> It is not a somber or depressing saying, but rather a reality that we have something greater to look forward to.
>
> Our center of our hearts is the Lord and the reason to live is Him. He fulfills every longing in us.
>
> Death has no sting for us. It is an absolute gain because we transcend in an instant from this world to the next.

Prayer: Lord I thank you for this amazing salvation and that being born again has started a new life in me that will not end while I follow after you. I can expect eternity and all the blessings both here and now and even after I pass on to the next life you have planned and prepared for me. Amen.

May 10

Colossians 3:13 "Bear with each other and forgive one another if any of you has a grievance against someone. Forgive as the Lord forgave you." NIV

> The Kingdom of God is hinged on forgiveness - we need forgiveness to be able to enter and become part of the Kingdom of God.
>
> It is essential for spiritual health to be able to forgive others.
>
> The quality of forgiveness is to forgive completely. We may not keep it in remembrance or discuss it or ever refer to it again. Once it is forgiven it no longer exists.

Prayer: Father I thank you that you have forgiven me and removed my sin as far as the east is from the west. Help me to completely forgive all those who have offended me in the past and in the future. Amen.

May 11

Mark 14:38 "Watch and pray so that you will not fall into temptation. The spirit is willing, but the flesh is weak." NIV

Following the example and lifestyle of Jesus would be to live a life of consistent prayer.

If we watch and pray then there is an atitude of being diligently alert in the spirit.

We have to recognize that though we may have good intentions (our spirit is willing), our natural nature is weak and therefore we need to be alert spiritually for temptation and stumbling.

Prayer: I thank you Lord Jesus that you set a wonderful example of prayer. Help me to be diligent and faithful in my prayer. Lord by your spirit I ask you to help me to watch and to be alert at all times that I will not fall into temptation of any kind. Amen.

May 12

Colossians 2:6-7 "So then, just as you received Christ Jesus as Lord, continue to live your lives in him, rooted and built up in him, strengthened in the faith as you were taught, and overflowing with thankfulness." NIV

> Once we become His then we continue to live in Him and we are rooted in Him.
>
> Through teaching and receiving the Word we are strengthened in our faith and,
>
> Especially when we practice thankfulness - thankfulness is the beginning of humility that the Lord so enjoys.

Prayer: I give you thanks for all that you have done and are doing for me Lord. I ask you to help me to stay thankful before you and to be built in my faith, established by you. Amen.

May 13

Ephesians 2:8-9 "For it is by grace you have been saved, through faith—and this is not from yourselves, it is the gift of God-not by works, so that no one can boast." NIV

> We need constant reminding that it is by grace that we are saved.
>
> And then grace and faith are inseparable and shake hands. We are saved by faith.
>
> It is an absolute gift of God and none of the works or our own efforts are able to secure our salvation - only the Lord.

Prayer: Father, this morning I rejoice in this tremendous salvation that I have received as a gift. Help me to always remember that it is just by your grace and not my works that I am able to find salvation. Amen.

May 14

Hebrews 4:15 "For we do not have a high priest who is unable to empathize with our weaknesses, but we have one who has been tempted in every way, just as we are—yet he did not sin." NIV

> We have a high priest - someone interceding and petitioning for us - always on our behalf so that we are secure.
>
> He has sympathy and understanding for our weaknesses and struggles;
>
> Yet this kindness and grace doesn't excuse a continuation in sin as He was without sin.

Prayer: Lord I thank you for your kindness and tolerance for my constant failures and weaknesses. I thank you for your grace that gives me the ability to overcome these things and to grow in you. By your grace I am more than a victor! Amen.

May 15

Romans 5:1 "Therefore, since we have been justified through faith, we have peace with God through our Lord Jesus Christ," NIV

> Our justification (being made right with God) is totally by faith.
>
> It is only through Jesus Christ and no other way.
>
> We can enjoy peace - the peace of God which is incomparable to anything in this world.

Prayer: Lord I thank you for your salvation that I am justified and I have faith in you and this salvation. I thank you for your peace today. Amen.

May 16

Micah 7:19 "You will again have compassion on us; you will tread our sins underfoot and hurl all our iniquities into the depths of the sea." NIV

> The nature of God is slow to anger and compassionate - now that we have the blood on the mercy seat it is even more times increased!
>
> God, by His nature and kindness, will tread our sins under foot individually and even as a nation when we call on Him.
>
> All we have to do is call and appeal to the Lord and He will answer and take away all our inequities, putting them in the depths of the sea.

Prayer: Lord I praise you for your greatness and your unending mercy and compassion for us. Thank you for forgiving me all my sins. And I pray for our nation today and all those around me that you will show mercy and forgiveness and pour your blessings on this nation and those around me. Amen.

May 17

Philippians 4:12 "I know what it is to be in need, and I know what it is to have plenty. I have learned the secret of being content in any and every situation, whether well fed or hungry, whether living in plenty or in want." NIV

Often in our lives we have diverse situations that influence our feeling of well being and that means our circumstances can dictate how we feel.

But we learn that it is not by these things that we learn contentment but by complete trust and relationship in Him.

Paul calls it a "secret" which is a great blessing to have this state where we learn to be content.

Prayer: I thank you Lord that I can be content in you and that my joy comes from knowing you. You are my source and supply and I am not moved or influenced by my circumstances. Amen.

May 18

Habakkuk 3:19 "The Sovereign Lord is my strength; he makes my feet like the feet of a deer, he enables me to tread on the heights." NIV

We do not have much strength on our own. We depend totally on Him - we can do ALL things through Christ who strengthens us.

He makes us like hind speed in high places that have very careful footing in very high elevated spots - The Lord watches over us and enables us even in tricky situations.

And the Lord is definitely our strength, we can depend on Him today and every day.

Prayer: Lord I thank you for your strength and your blessing on my life today. Give me courage to face the things that are ahead of me with great joy and confidence, knowing you will give me a sure foot even in difficult situations. I will not stumble. Amen.

May 19

Luke 6:45 "A good man brings good things out of the good stored up in his heart, and an evil man brings evil things out of the evil stored up in his heart. For the mouth speaks what the heart is full of." NIV

The evidence is clear - what comes out of the mouth of a person reflects what's inside.

Changing only the speech is not enough because under pressure the real part will show. It is necessary to adjust the heart.

Not everything coming out of the mouth came from the heart, sometimes we are foolish and careless with our mouths and we ought to take care with those things too.

Prayer: Father I give you full permission to change my heart, to renew the right spirit in me so when the overflow comes out of my mouth it reflects only that which is good. I want to be the good man, not the evil man. Amen.

May 20

Acts 20:22 "And now, compelled by the Spirit, I am going to Jerusalem, not knowing what will happen to me there." NIV

Compelled - there was a urgency in his heart - there was no blinding light or angelic appearance; often our leading of the Lord is just a mere "gut" feeling.

Not knowing - God often moves and directs us with limited knowledge of the future and He expects us to trust Him that we will arrive at His purpose and plan that He destined for us.

There is something that waits for us in doing the purposes of God.

Prayer: Lord help me to respond to your commands and obey you to reach the destiny you have planned for me. Help me to trust in you without knowing everything. Amen.

May 21

Revelation 2:3 "You have persevered and have endured hardships for my name, and have not grown weary." NIV

> The only beneficial hardships for us are those we endure because and for the Lord.
>
> The Lord commends us when we do not grow weary and endure with a good attitude and confident spirit.
>
> We ought not to give up but to endure because those that endure to the end shall be saved!

Prayer: Father I ask you to help me today to have a right attitude and to persevere through things that seem to be less than pleasant. Help me to keep the goal in mind to see the crown of glory as an overcomer. I need your strength to do this today because without you I can do nothing. Amen.

May 22

1 Corinthians 12:31 "Now eagerly desire the greater gifts. And yet I will show you the most excellent way." NIV

It is God's purpose and wish that we "desire" spiritual gifts; so that we can be a blessing to other people.

We should desire the greater gifts, which would be the gifts that are life changing for other people.

But there is a more excellent way and that is the way of love. Only God is love and can produce true love.

Prayer: Lord I do desire spiritual gifts, especially the ones that are more effective in people's lives. I pray that you fill me and teach this more excellent way that I may be a vessel of love every day to all people. Amen.

May 23

Philippians 3:13 "Brothers and sisters, I do not consider myself yet to have taken hold of it. But one thing I do: Forgetting what is behind and straining toward what is ahead" NIV

Forgetting what is behind - we cannot live in the past, there is no life there. His name is I am not I was.

Straining toward what is ahead - regardless how difficult the future may seem, we press toward the future rather than trying to fix the past.

We cannot change the past but we can improve our future by giving God full control of our lives.

Prayer: Lord I praise you for your kindness and mercy toward me. Reflecting back I know you have shown me mercy. I ask you to help me to press onto the mark, not living in the past but working toward the future. By your love and grace, Amen.

May 24

Psalm 62:1 "Truly my soul finds rest in God; my salvation comes from him." NIV

There is no rest that compares to rest that God gives us. It is a wonderful gift in a turmoil life.

God alone is our solution to any situation - nobody can deliver or give peace like the Lord.

My salvation comes from Him - there is no other salvation or way to eternal life except through Jesus and our almighty God.

Prayer: Father I thank you for your amazing salvation and I claim the rest you have promised me that I will walk in peace and find rest in you and not be anxious for anything. Amen.

May 25

John 6:27 "Do not work for food that spoils, but for food that endures to eternal life, which the Son of Man will give you. For on him God the Father has placed his seal of approval." NIV

> We ought to pursue things with more energy that are eternal - they far outweigh the earthly things.
>
> If we pursue supernatural things our rewards continue forever and will not be a short momentary situation.
>
> Eternal life comes from the son, which He gives us as a free gift. God has put His seal of approval on Him.

Prayer: Father thank you for this wonderful salvation that you have given me and my family. I ask you Lord to help me to pursue the things that have more eternal value and not to focus all my energy on things of this world. Amen.

May 26

Colossians 4:6 "Let your conversation be always full of grace, seasoned with salt, so that you may know how to answer everyone." NIV

> Jesus said it is not what goes in but what comes out of the mouth that defiles.
>
> When we speak we ought to use wisdom and take great care that we speak with kindness and life and not say anything we would later regret.
>
> When we answer people we should ask God for wisdom that our speech is full grace.

Prayer: Lord I ask that you take full control over my mouth and the words I speak that they may bring life to others and bring glory to you. Amen.

May 27

1 Corinthians 10:31 "So whether you eat or drink or whatever you do, do it all for the glory of God." NIV

> Our lives are full of things that seemingly have no value, but we are required to do it for the Lord.
>
> Our hearts and minds are focused on glorifying God. In everything we do we take care and consider how we may glorify Him in doing that.
>
> Our lives are not our own, He has bought us and so everything we are and do belongs to Him.

Prayer: Lord I recommit my heart and life to you. Direct my path I pray, and help me to do everything I do today for your glory. Help me to consider carefully how I do them that I may bring glory to your name. Amen.

May 28

Hebrews 11:1 "Now faith is confidence in what we hope for and assurance about what we do not see." NIV

> We hope, because the Lord is faithful and we have reasonable hope that He will do good towards us.
>
> Our faith comes from hearing the Word and He gives us security and surety to what we are hoping for.
>
> And then it grows in us to become certain, even if we do not see it or until we see it.

Prayer: I thank you Lord for increasing faith in me by hearing your word. Help me to be responsible in every way by walking in faith and your obedience today. Amen.

May 29

Romans 6:14 "For sin shall no longer be your master, because you are not under the law, but under grace." NIV

> We were slaves to sin before we were saved. Now we are free not to sin - or free even, to sin. There is a choice.
>
> No sin can master us because we are now free through Christ and we ought to walk in that freedom and not sin.
>
> We are under grace, which is God's divine favor. We will not be condemned because of His goodness.

Prayer: Lord, I thank you for your grace and that you have saved me. I thank you father that it's the same grace that saves me, that gives me the ability to overcome sin and do what is right in your sight. I praise you for goodness and love. Help me to continue to walk in it. In Jesus name, Amen.

May 30

Matthew 6:20-21 "But store up for yourselves treasures in heaven, where moths and vermin do not destroy, and where thieves do not break in and steal. For where your treasure is, there your heart will be also." NIV

Treasure is something that we hold to ourselves as precious and where our treasure is our heart follows naturally. If we follow the money, how we spend it, we can find out what is really important to us.

It is important that we get things in perspective, focus and invest more in eternal things than things of this world. In heaven there is no losing what we invest.

It is all about our heart - that our heart be invested in Him and His Kingdom more than all other things. There is nothing wrong with having "stuff" as long as we love Him much more.

Prayer: Father I thank you for all that You do for me in the natural. Help me to focus my energy and my life in things that are eternal and to have my heart in the right place, Your Kingdom. Amen.

May 31

2 Corinthians 1:20 "For no matter how many promises God has made, they are "Yes" in Christ. And so through him the "Amen" is spoken by us to the glory of God." NIV

Unlike man God keeps His promise.

We can depend upon Him no matter what things look like because God always comes through with His promises and what He says.

The enemy does whatever He can to try and discourage our confidence in His promises and we ought to refresh ourselves daily on what He actually said and not get confused about His promises.

Prayer: Father thank you for your promises and your word that is always true. Help me to refresh myself in what you have promised and to believe and expect exactly what you said. Amen.

June 1

Matthew 20:26 "whoever wants to become great among you must be your servant, and whoever wants to be first must be your slave" NIV

> Having goals are wonderful but selfish ambition can often be confused with those things.
>
> Our goal should be to please the Lord and not to try and be great for our own benefit.
>
> The Lord says we are great when we are servants of all.

Prayer: Father create in me the right servant heart that I can serve others and always have joy doing it because I want to be like you and please you. You are the love of my life. Amen.

June 2

2 Timothy 1:7 "For the Spirit God gave us does not make us timid, but gives us power, love and self-discipline." NIV

> Fear is directly from the devil - we must resist it all times.
>
> We have a sound mind that God has given us. In fact, we have the mind of Christ!
>
> We need to remind ourselves when fear knocks on the door what the Lord has promised us and who we are in Him.

Prayer: Thank you Lord for the power, love and sound mind you have given me. Help me to resist fear at all times and walk in confidence that you are unchanging. Amen.

June 3

Lamentations 3:25-26 "The Lord is good to those whose hope is in him, to the one who seeks him;it is good to wait quietly for the salvation of theLord." NIV

> Waiting for Him is to be focused on the Lord and seeking Him is a whole attitude of always wanting Him.
>
> The promise is that He will bless and do us "good".
>
> The Lord has a solution and He wants us to be patient and quietly waiting until He comes and breaks through for us. Hallelujah!

Prayer: Lord today I choose to be quietly waiting, full of confidence and hope, that you will rescue me from my situation. Help me to help others and to encourage them in their plights too. Amen.

June 4

James 1:22 "Do not merely listen to the word, and so deceive yourselves. Do what it says." NIV

> First, we often have difficulty hearing some of the things God says;
>
> But then to become actual doers that carry out what He says, seems to be a continual life challenge.
>
> David was recognized by God as a man after His own heart because He did what God said. (Acts 13:22)

Prayer: Lord I ask you to give me the strength and tenacity today to do exactly what you say, the courage to hear you clearly and to obey. Amen.

June 5

Proverbs 25:28 "A man who cannot rule his own spirit is like a city whose walls are broken down." NLV

>Self control is one of the nine fruits of the Holy Spirit and very little talked about.

>Self discipline takes practice even in the small daily things and doing it even when you don't feel like it.

>Self discipline is especially required when we don't want to do something. If we wanted to do it we wouldn't need self discipline - it would be too easy.

Prayer: Lord I submit my heart and soul to you. I ask you to develop the self discipline in my life to do what I know is right and pleasing in your sight, even when I am not in the mood for it. Amen.

June 6

Luke 16:10 "Whoever can be trusted with very little can also be trusted with much, and whoever is dishonest with very little will also be dishonest with much." NIV

Being faithful is a very godly attribute and everyone longs for a faithful friend or family member. God wants us to be faithful to what He has committed to us.

He first tries us in the smaller things and if we can't do that then He is not going to trust us with the bigger things. So we have to make an effort to do what even seems sometimes demeaning or of no importance, but be faithful.

We should aspire to do the greater things for the Lord by simply doing the small ones first and be excited to be trusted with the greater treasures of the Lord.

Prayer: Father I love you and all that I do is for you. Help me to be faithful in every little thing to show you that I am faithful and that my heart desires to please you in every way. Amen.

June 7

Joshua 1:7 "Be strong and very courageous. Be careful to obey all the law my servant Moses gave you; do not turn from it to the right or to the left, that you may be successful wherever you go." NIV

> Being strong and courageous means that there is always a challenge up ahead and we should not cower or be fearful in the face of it.
>
> We are to, according to the "law of Moses" which means to simply adhere to the pleasures and purposes of God, put Him first in our hearts and consider His ways.
>
> Jesus did say that if we love Him we will keep His commandments. We can expect that He will prosper and bless us in all of our ways when we make an effort to do what He asks us.

Prayer: Lord I thank you for the spirit of courage today to face whatever is ahead of me and not to cower. Let your ways and your word be my platform to work from. Thank you Holy Spirit that you remind me of His promises and His direction every day. Amen.

June 8

Psalm 145:18 "The Lord is near to all who call on him, to all who call on him in truth." NIV

God responds when we call! Just a simple call. Unlike us who do not respond sometimes to phone calls, He is waiting for our call and He responds instantly.

He does draw near to us when we call to Him and we must expect that even when might not feel it.

We ought to call upon Him in truth, which means from a place of sincerity, not just casually or flippantly.

Prayer: Lord I thank you that when I call upon you I can expect you to answer. I am so grateful that you would be mindful of me who is just a human. You are such a great God and I praise you for it. Amen.

June 9

Luke 1:37 "For with God nothing will be impossible." NKJ

> Nothing means nothing! There is absolutely no limit.
>
> God is not only able, but He is willing to do if we can just believe in Him and ask of Him.
>
> God specializes in the impossible - what we think is so impossible is so easy for the Lord.

Prayer: Lord today I make a clear decision to believe for the impossible even if it is difficult. I trust in you and expecting you to do a miracle because I am asking by faith because you are the God of the impossible. Thank you for making a way where there seems to be no way. I praise you for it. Amen.

June 10

Jeremiah 17:10 "I the Lord search the heart and examine the mind, to reward each person according to their conduct, according to what their deeds deserve." NIV

God definitely searches our heart and the motives of our heart and we ought to make sure we understand it.

God tests our mind and our hearts and make sure that we are right and He rewards us according to the things we do.

We ought to be convinced in our heart that what we sow or what we are doing is going to effect our lives and eternity. God is certainly watching and observing what we do and checking our hearts and motives.

Prayer: Father help me to keep my heart and attitude right and to do what is pleasing in your site. I am weak but you are strong so I look to you today for my strength to do everything according to your purpose and plan. Amen.

June 11

2 Peter 3:9 "The Lord is not slack concerning His promise, as some count slackness, but is long suffering toward us, not willing that any should perish but that all should come to repentance." NIV

Sometimes because of the long wait we think that God is not taking care of His promises, but He does keep His word!

He is very patient and is waiting for us to see if we are right before we encounter His dealings. He is so patient with us and those around us that seem (in our minds) to need immediate adjustments.

The way of the Lord is full of mercy and kindness that we enjoy and we ought to allow others to also benefit from that same mercy and kindness.

Prayer: Father I thank you for your goodness and mercy towards me. Help me to have that same spirit towards others and not to be frustrated because your promises do not happen fast enough. I praise you that you do keep your word. Amen.

June 12

1 Peter 2:9 "But you are a chosen generation, a royal priesthood, a holy nation, His own special people, that you may proclaim the praises of Him who called you out of darkness into His marvelous light;" NIV

> We are chosen - We did not choose Him, He chose us!
>
> People that belong to Him are dedicated to Him and represent Him.
>
> As His people we need to declare to the world and pull whatever is in the darkness into the light.

Prayer: Thank you Lord for calling us a chosen people and for choosing me. Help me to daily reflect you so that others may see you in me and be drawn to you. Amen.

June 13

1 Chronicles 29:11 "Yours, O Lord, is the greatness, The power and the glory, The victory and the majesty; For all that is in heaven and in earth is Yours; Yours is the kingdom, O Lord, And You are exalted as head over all." NIV

When we observe and take in all that goes on around us we forget that it all belongs to the Almighty God.

We that know Him and have a relationship with Him are convinced and are sure that He is on the throne and that all He has promised will come to pass.

We see the kings and leaders of the world doing what they do and wonder, but we know that even the heart of the king is in the hand of God.

Prayer: Lord I praise you this day because the earth and the heavens are yours and I belong to you. I am safe in your hands knowing you are sovereign and your will will be done. Amen.

June 14

Hebrews 13:8 "Jesus Christ is the same yesterday and today and forever." NIV

When we read a 2000 year old account of Jesus we often picture Him as a savior of those days and in actual fact He is unchanged.

We easily forget our resolve (things we have decided) when our life situations change, not realizing that what Jesus said then still holds true today.

He is unchanging - we can depend on everything He says, His consistency and His great love.

Prayer: Lord I praise you that you are unchanging and I can depend upon you and all your promises no matter what it looks like today. Amen.

June 15

Psalm 103:1 "Praise the Lord, my soul; all my inmost being, praise his holy name." NIV

> It is our calling to praise and worship Him as He said that if we don't praise Him the stones would cry His praise.
>
> We tell our soul and innermost being to praise Him because we don't always feel the unction to do it.
>
> His name is holy, unblemished and beautiful. The whole world knows His name and every knee will bow at His name one day.

Prayer: Lord I praise you and I ask you to put the spirit of praise and thanksgiving in my heart daily so that I may give you the worship you deserve. Amen.

June 16

Hebrews 10:23 Let us hold unswervingly to the hope we profess, for he who promised is faithful. NIV

> Not swerving - not to be even slightly distracted or discouraged. Holding on and not giving up.
>
> Hope - a positive expectancy. It is this positive expectancy that we share with others.
>
> God never fails and we can be sure He will not let us down no matter what our situation looks like today!

Prayer: Father I thank you for this hope of eternal life and all the promises You have given me. I praise You that I can focus on these continually. Amen.

June 17

1 Thessalonians 4:13 "Brothers and sisters, we do not want you to be uninformed about those who sleep in death, so that you do not grieve like the rest of mankind, who have no hope." NIV

>Natural death is imminent for all.

>We don't grieve or feel the hopelessness as other people do because we are assured of eternity.

>Death has no sting for us because we have the promise that we will transcend in a split second into life. (John 11:25)

Prayer: Praise you Lord! Father I thank you for the assurance of eternity and that this life holds no fear of death or end. Help me to live a life full of hope and expectancy. Amen.

June 18

Philippians 4:8 "Finally, brothers and sisters, whatever is true, whatever is noble, whatever is right, whatever is pure, whatever is lovely, whatever is admirable—if anything is excellent or praiseworthy—think about such things." NIV

> The war is in our minds - it is very easy to dwell on negative things about people and situations but the fruit of it is so destructive.
>
> It's a choice - we must make a choice to think on the right things that our minds can be focused on what is good that we develop wholeness in our souls.
>
> Scriptures talk about taking thoughts "captive" so we must control what we spend our time thinking about.

Prayer: Father I submit my thought life to you and ask you to direct my thoughts to all that is good and pure. Amen.

June 19

Isaiah 55:11 "so is my word that goes out from my mouth: It will not return to me empty, but will accomplish what I desire and achieve the purpose for which I sent it." NIV

God sends His word. His word is like an arrow shot at a target.

God promises us in return without any effect the word will do what it says - All God's promises, demands and prophecies He has spoken will be accomplished.

God's word is always life and it cannot be stopped, not even in the worst of circumstances.

Prayer: Lord I praise you for your word. Help me to continually believe and expect your words to come to pass. Amen.

June 20

Psalms 36:7 "How priceless is your unfailing love, O God! People take refuge in the shadow of your wings." NIV

> Love that never fails - no matter what, God's love continues towards us. Regardless of what we've done wrong or failed to do right, He loves us!
>
> All men everywhere and in every walk in life, saved and unsaved, are able to enjoy His love.
>
> We are sheltered in the goodness of God even if we don't deserve it. His love is like wings that cover us.

Prayer: Lord I praise you today from the bottom of my heart for your great love that never fails regardless of my failings. I thank you Father that there is no greater love than yours. Amen.

June 21

2 Corinthians 2:14 "But thanks be to God, who always leads us as captives in Christ's triumphal procession and uses us to spread the aroma of the knowledge of him everywhere." NIV

> We have this confidence that the target is always a triumph! No matter what we face or go through the end product is triumphant because of His promise. We can expect it.
>
> It is a procession - meaning that there are others. All those that follow Christ and trust in Him that are full of triumph in a victorious, overcoming celebration.
>
> Fragrance is something that is unavoidable for people to smell - so they will not deny the knowledge of Him through our triumph and victory as we walk in the procession with the Lord.

Prayer: Lord I thank you for the triumph and victory you have promised us. I focus my heart and attention on you today for you are my helper and strength. Amen.

June 22

Luke 6:35 "But love your enemies, do good to them, and lend to them without expecting to get anything back. Then your reward will be great, and you will be children of the Most High, because he is kind to the ungrateful and wicked." NIV

> Loving enemies is more of a challenge than we often expect because the enemy is someone who deliberately does us harm. It is only by His grace and power that helps us to actually love them.
>
> The principle of giving and not expecting back brings us back to being recognized as His children because we don't operate as the world.
>
> God is actually kind to the ungrateful and wicked - how amazing is that?

Prayer: Lord who is there like you that is actually kind to wicked people? I ask you today to help me to be a representative of you and have your heart and nature even toward the ungrateful and wicked. Amen.

June 23

John 15:15 "I no longer call you servants, because a servant does not know his master's business. Instead, I have called you friends, for everything that I learned from my Father I have made known to you." NIV

> What a honor that we be called His friend, or on such a level that He would value us in such a way.
>
> We are to know His "business" - that which the Lord is doing and the work of His hands.
>
> He reveals to us as He learns from the Father - as we stay close to Him in relationship, we will always be up-to-date with what the Lord wants from us.

Prayer: Lord I thank you so much for calling me a friend. Your love and grace is beyond my understanding. Help me to always be alert and attentive to your leading so I'm aware of where we're going and how I can participate in your plan today. Amen.

June 24

Revelation 3:20 "Here I am! I stand at the door and knock. If anyone hears my voice and opens the door, I will come in and eat with that person, and they with me." NIV

> The Lord is always ready to come and fellowship with us if we will just open up to Him. We are not waiting for HIm, He is waiting for us.
>
> If we hear His voice - we ought to be paying attention and not resist HIm.
>
> It is a mutual "eating" - which means of sharing and communing together.

Prayer: Lord help me to be alert when you knock at the door and hear your voice so that I can fellowship with you. I long for your presence in my life and so enjoy your goodness and love. Help me to share this with others today. Amen.

June 25

James 2:20 "You foolish person, do you want evidence that faith without deeds is useless?" NIV

We have learned that faith without works is dead. That means that something has to be "done" for there to be evidence and to complete the step of faith.

It would be foolish to look for the evidence - one is inseparable from the other as history shows it through leaders throughout the world and God's kingdom.

Faith produces works - we will "do" something when we believe God and not just wait.

Prayer: Lord I do not need evidence that faith without works has no life. Help me today to be responsive to your purpose in faith and do all that you ask of me. I declare that without you I am nothing. I bless your name today Lord. Amen.

June 26

Isaiah 40:11 "He tends his flock like a shepherd: He gathers the lambs in his arms and carries them close to his heart; he gently leads those that have young." NIV

> We are the sheep of His pasture and He is truly the good shepherd!
>
> We can be safe in the arms of our Lord as He watches over us day and night like a good shepherd does.
>
> He holds us close to His heart and leads us with gentleness - that is how important we are to Him.

Prayer: I praise you Lord that you are the good shepherd and that you watch over me today and that I can feel safe regardless where I find myself. Thank you for taking care of me. Amen.

June 27

Hebrews 13:21 "equip you with everything good for doing his will, and may he work in us what is pleasing to him, through Jesus Christ, to whom be glory for ever and ever. Amen." NIV

> God equips those He calls and equips us for what we need - to do His will.
>
> We all want Him to work in us and bring us to a place that is pleasing in HIs sight.
>
> And it is all through Jesus Christ because He is not just our covering but our redeemer and savior. God looks at the mercy seat and sees the lamb. We are in Him and safe.

Prayer: Lord I ask you to equip me with everything I need that is good so I may do your will today effectively and fruitfully. I desire to be and do what is pleasing in your sight in everything I do. I give you glory for it in Jesus name. Amen.

June 28

Matthew 6:15 "But if you do not forgive others their sins, your Father will not forgive your sins." NIV

The whole kingdom of God hinges on forgiveness - we receive complete forgiveness and we ought to give complete forgiveness.

Penalty for refusing or withholding forgiveness is that we are also denied from the Father of our forgiveness.

The severity of forgiveness needs to press home to all of us. To release all those that have offended us in every shape and form completely that we may receive our complete forgiveness.

Prayer: Lord I pray for a spirit of forgiveness in my heart to continually forgive, not only those in the past but as people offend me now. Help me to always be in a state of mind of forgiveness that I may continue to receive forgiveness from you. Fill me with your spirit and you love today I pray. Amen.

June 29

Matthew 4:4 "Jesus answered, "It is written: 'Man shall not live on bread alone, but on every word that comes from the mouth of God.'" NIV

> The body needs sustenance, natural food but our spirits and souls need something that only comes from heaven.
>
> His Word is life and light. All those that serve Him are unable to survive or live without His words.
>
> Even those around us who are not in relationship with Him need His words of life and we ought to be vessels of those words.

Prayer: Lord make me an instrument of your words of life that I may bring life to those around me and draw them closer to you. I give myself to you today especially for that. Amen.

June 30

2 Peter 1:5-7 "In view of all this, make every effort to respond to God's promises. Supplement your faith with a generous provision of moral excellence, and moral excellence with knowledge, and knowledge with self-control, and self-control with patient endurance, and patient endurance with godliness, and godliness with brotherly affection, and brotherly affection with love for everyone." NLT

Christian nature is an ongoing development and progress.

As we grow in faith we must make an effort to add all these christlike and fruitful attributes on a daily basis.

It is imperative we understand how the Lord view us in relationship to others that He wants us to treat them with utmost care and love.

Prayer: Father fill me with your spirit and help me to add all these attributes to my faith on a continual basis that I may become a testament of your goodness and bring glory to you in everything I do and say. Amen.

July 1

Psalm 62:7 "My salvation and my honor depend on God; he is my mighty rock, my refuge." NIV

> All our solutions for life's challenges come from Him.
>
> All that we are and ever could be finds it's origin in the Lord and His grace towards me.
>
> We can take refuge in Him no matter what our situation is because He is an unchanging "rock".

Prayer: Lord I praise you today that you are my refuge and my rock and that I can look to you to rescue me and help me. I can expect it because of your promises. Amen.

July 2

2 Thessalonians 3:3 "But the Lord is faithful, and he will strengthen you and protect you from the evil one." NIV

One thing is for sure - God never changes and He can be depended upon. All men make mistakes and fail but God never fails!

We can expect Him to strengthen us when we feel frail and almost desperate. We know that He will help us.

The enemy is real but God promises to protect us and we ought to embrace that.

Prayer: Lord I thank you that you are my shield and protector from the evil one. I look to you today to strengthen me that I can be all that you desire me to be. Amen.

July 3

1 Peter 5:10 "And the God of all grace, who called you to his eternal glory in Christ, after you have suffered a little while, will himself restore you and make you strong, firm and steadfast." NIV

God is certainly the god of all grace - undeserved favor, unwarranted, but oh so amazing!

The glory that we share with our Lord Jesus through redemption is eternal.

In this life we do have sufferings and difficulties but it is so short and His restoration is imminent and promised to us.

Prayer: Father I thank you for your amazing grace that is always abounding to me. I ask that you fill me with your spirit today so that I will not focus on the sufferings but on the restoration you promised and eternal glory that waits. Amen.

July 4

Deuteronomy 33:27 "The eternal God is your refuge, and underneath are the everlasting arms." NIV

> A refuge is a place we can run to and find cover - that is our God.
>
> Often His arms are depicted as wings or coverings and we can be sheltered from all violent attacks under His arms. It's something we can be sure of.
>
> He undergirds us, He lifts us up and upholds us in the worst of times.

Prayer: Lord I praise you that you are my refuge and that I can run to you knowing that you will lift me up, cover me and protect me today. Help me to focus on how great you are and not any difficulties around me. Amen.

July 5

Psalm 37:4 "Take delight in the Lord, and he will give you the desires of your heart." NIV

>Delighting in the Lord is putting Him first as the love of our lives and enjoying Him more than anything else.

>And He gives gladly the desires - not what we want - but rather putting the right desires inside of us.

>When our heart is focused on Him, we desire the right things and He often leads us by those very same desires.

Prayer: Lord I do choose to delight in you and put my joy and expectancy in you. I trust that you will give me the right desires today that I can be all that you desire me to be. I praise you for your goodness and mercy. Amen.

July 6

*1 John 2:6 "Whoever claims to live in him must live as Jesus did."
NIV*

It is important for us to identify and claim to be His disciple and follower.

As we claim that we have to reflect Him, which is no easy task in the natural. But God gives us the grace and the power.

Our focus is to walk and behave as Jesus did as we follow Him, rather than the expectancy of men.

Prayer: Lord I thank you for saving me. Help me to become like you and to reflect you in every way of my behavior and talk that I can really be your representative. Amen.

July 7

Hebrews 10:22 "let us draw near to God with a sincere heart and with the full assurance that faith brings, having our hearts sprinkled to cleanse us from a guilty conscience and having our bodies washed with pure water." NIV

We must, ourselves, draw near to Him so that He can draw near to us - it is our effort first.

It is by faith that we come to Him with our hearts that is sprinkled with His goodness, love, mercy and His blood that we can have a clear conscience from all our sin.

We are saved by faith and not our own works. Our heavenly/spiritual bodies are washed with pure water which is Christ Jesus himself.

Prayer: Lord I do draw near to you because of the completed work of Jesus. Thank you for this great salvation. Amen.

July 8

2 Timothy 4:18 "The Lord will rescue me from every evil attack and will bring me safely to his heavenly kingdom. To him be glory for ever and ever. Amen." NIV

God does rescue - especially when we so often are in need and need a helping hand.

Just like any rescuer in a storm they have to bring us to a place of safety - so will God also bring us safely into His Kingdom.

There is a wonderful assurance that there is always a capable rescuer - our Lord Jesus!

Prayer: Thank you Lord that you will rescue me and that I have nothing to fear but fear itself. I ask you to strengthen my innermost being and my faith that I will confidence that you will rescue me today. Amen.

July 9

Romans 2:29 "No, a person is a Jew who is one inwardly; and circumcision is circumcision of the heart, by the Spirit, not by the written code. Such a person's praise is not from other people, but from God." NIV

Being a Jew means to be "chosen". Since we are adopted through salvation into the family of God we are chosen and are actual Jews, more than just physical, but spiritually.

Circumcision was a sign for people dedicated to God and God called us to have a circumcision of heart, which means a different attitude and spirit from inside rather than the outward.

When we do these things we have God's approval and praise.

Prayer: Lord, how I praise you for saving me and circumcision of heart you have done inside of me. I ask you to continue to grow me in your ways that I might become, in every way, a reflection of you. Amen.

July 10

Matthew 5:30 "And if your right hand causes you to stumble, cut it off and throw it away. It is better for you to lose one part of your body than for your whole body to go into hell." NIV

We are no longer slaves to sin, we are free because what the Son of God has made free is free indeed.

We ought to make every effort to avoid falling into sin or doing things that are wrong, even if it means making some severe adjustments.

There is a cost to be paid for continuing in sin. The cost of making serious adjustments always outweighs the cost of losing everything.

Prayer: Lord I commit my heart and life to you and ask you to lead me in the way that is right and pure. Keep me from all temptation as you taught me to pray. I ask you to give me wisdom of what things to avoid that will cause me to fall. Amen.

July 11

2 Corinthians 13:5 "Examine yourselves to see whether you are in the faith; test yourselves. Do you not realize that Christ Jesus is in you—unless, of course, you fail the test?" NIV

> It is God's requirement that we truthfully examine our own hearts - that means to look at the motives and reasons why we do things.
>
> To see whether we do things that are in the faith - which means complete dependency on the Lord and not for selfish or foolish reasons.
>
> As we examine ourselves we should see the evidence of the Lord living inside of us, helping us making the right decisions and keeping a right attitude.

Prayer: Lord I ask your Holy Spirit to help me examine my heart that I am truthful with myself and see that my motivations are always correct and that my attitude is right in everything I do. I am totally yours and want to follow you with all of my heart. Amen.

July 12

John 16:23 "In that day you will no longer ask me anything. Very truly I tell you, my Father will give you whatever you ask in my name." NIV

>Because of this wonderful salvation and sacrifice of our Lord Jesus Christ we are able to call our Father "Abba Father".
>
>And we have the right to ask anything - Jesus did say "whatever" and he would give us what we ask for.
>
>It is a wonderful privilege and blessing to have this liberty to ask in His name because of the completed work of our Lord Jesus.

Prayer: Lord I praise you today and thank you for this amazing salvation and goodness that I have this right to call you father and are able to ask you anything. I bless and praise you. Amen.

July 13

1 Peter 1:5 "who through faith are shielded by God's power until the coming of the salvation that is ready to be revealed in the last time." NIV

> The shield of faith protects us from attacks on our salvation or hope in Christ.
>
> God is all powerful and His power is able to shield us from anything and we should depend on that.
>
> The salvation that is going to be revealed is the returning of our Lord Jesus, which we all agree is eminent.

Prayer: Father thank you that you are a shield and that your power protects me. I am weak but you are strong and I can rejoice today no matter what I am facing, for you are my helper and I thank you for it. Amen.

July 14

2 Peter 2:9 "if this is so, then the Lord knows how to rescue the godly from trials and to hold the unrighteous for punishment on the day of judgment." NIV

> We are godly because of the redemption of Christ and we can expect Him to rescue us from all trials.
>
> Judgment awaits those that refuse God or resist Him.
>
> Punishment is inevitable for those who are not in right standing or in relationship with the Lord and that is why we should do all we can to share this gospel that there may be none lost.

Prayer: Lord I thank you for rescuing me and saving my soul even though I am unworthy. I was a sinner but yet you loved me and saved me. Help me to have the same heart and compassion for others that are not in right standing with you and help me to share this gospel with them. Amen.

July 15

Revelation 12:11 "They triumphed over him by the blood of the Lamb and by the word of their testimony; they did not love their lives so much as to shrink from death." NIV

Satan has been overcome and his work has been destroyed by the blood that was shed on calvary - Jesus' perfect and holy blood.

His blood and the word of our testimony, which is how we declare that He is our savior, and the works He has done renders the enemy powerless.

When the enemy comes against us we can depend upon the blood and the finished work that was done. We can speak continually the testimony in whom we trust and what we expect the Lord to do for us.

Prayer: Lord I thank you for this shed blood on calvary that cleanses me from all sin and has given me power against the enemy. Help me to continually testify of your greatness and let the word that I speak help overcome the works of the enemy in my life and the lives around me. Amen.

July 16

Philippians 1:21 "For to me, to live is Christ and to die is gain." NIV

> Living on this earth is to live for Him and to be effective and fruitful so that when we see Him face to face we will not be empty handed.
>
> For a true born again christian death is a wonderful and appealing event.
>
> The reality of belonging to Him, once born again, is life as Jesus said and even when we end this earthly life our lives continue with Him - this is a reality!

Prayer: Lord I confess today that I live for you and count it as a great privilege to do all that I do for you today. And Lord by your grace I thank you that there is no fear or concern of my natural life's end but rather an excitement to see you face to face. Amen.

July 17

Luke 8:13 "Those on the rocky ground are the ones who receive the word with joy when they hear it, but they have no root. They believe for a while, but in the time of testing they fall away." NIV

We are to be "rooted" in Christ - to have a sincere relationship with Him.

Hearing, believing and being excited about the Word isn't enough if we do not put it into practice or allow it to work in our lives.

Testing and trials are inevitable for all of us and it is how we will endure that is important. Without being rooted in Jesus and having that firm relationship it may prove too much for us to bare.

Prayer: Lord I thank you that I am rooted in you and that you have saved me. I receive your word with joy and thank you that it produces life in me. By your grace all the difficulties I face will not weaken me or take me away from serving you but instead increase my dependency and love for you. Amen.

July 18

Matthew 14:30 "But when he saw the wind, he was afraid and, beginning to sink, cried out, "Lord, save me!" NIV

It is the enemy's target to create fear by focussing us on the difficult situations.

In the beginning of sinking it is wise to cry out to the Lord because He will answer.

In calling Him to save us we can be sure He will rescue us even when we are distracted and have allowed fear to enter. He is still faithful.

Prayer: Lord I thank you that you are my savior and helper even when I am weak, you are strong. I cry to you today Lord and thank you that you help me in the face of difficulties and I have nothing to fear for you are my strength. Amen.

July 19

2 Samuel 7:25 "And now, Lord God, keep forever the promise you have made concerning your servant and his house. Do as you promised," NIV

God's promises are always true - They never fail!

He has made promises to us individually and corporately to our families that we can depend upon. Even when we are gone our descendants and family can still enjoy the benefits of these promises and blessings.

His promises are not dependent on our or our descendant's obedience - David's descendants, with their disobedience, still stayed on the throne because of God's promise.

Prayer: Lord I thank you for your promises that are true. Even when we fail to keep ours you are always faithful with your promises. Lord I pray for my family that you bless them and that your favor and blessing be upon them even after I am gone. In Jesus Name, Amen.

July 20

Isaiah 41:14 "Do not be afraid, you worm Jacob, little Israel, do not fear, for I myself will help you," declares the Lord, your Redeemer, the Holy One of Israel." NIV

> Even the weakest of us are great when God reaches out His hand - He described Jacob as a worm.
>
> God Himself steps in rather than sending ministering spirits to help us - He calls Himself our Redeemer!
>
> How blessed we are to have such a mighty God and Redeemer who takes time for even the smallest details of our lives.

Prayer: Father I praise you that you are my Redeemer and that I don't have to be afraid. Thank you for helping me today. Amen.

July 21

Romans 4:5 "However, to the one who does not work but trusts God who justifies the ungodly, their faith is credited as righteousness." NIV

> Dead works without faith does not produce life.
>
> It is by faith that we are justified and made righteous.
>
> Faith produces works that bring righteousness and fruitfulness.

Prayer: Lord I thank for this tremendous salvation that you gave us through Christ and that I am made righteous because of Him alone. And because of this wonderful salvation I choose to do what is right and productive for your name's sake. Amen.

July 22

Matthew 10:28 "Do not be afraid of those who kill the body but cannot kill the soul. Rather, be afraid of the One who can destroy both soul and body in hell." NIV

> We are not to be afraid - fear is not what we have received from the Lord but rather a spirit of love and power and a sound mind.
>
> The enemy tries to create fear in us of things around us and he tries to intimidate us, but we are not be afraid of natural things.
>
> We are to be aware and extra careful of the enemy that destroys our souls, or the spiritual things that are more eternal.

Prayer: Farther I pray that you help me not to fear what any man or any situation can do to me but rather to be more concerned about spiritual matters that are eternal. Help me to keep my focus on these things. Amen.

July 23

1 Corinthians 1:3-4 "Praise be to the God and Father of our Lord Jesus Christ, the Father of compassion and the God of all comfort, who comforts us in all our troubles, so that we can comfort those in any trouble with the comfort we ourselves receive from God." NIV

The Lord is truly a comforter. The Holy Spirit is called 'The Comforter' and we can really rely on Him to comfort us in every situation.

God is a god of compassion and He comforts us so that we can comfort others.

We are to be unselfish and kind to those that are struggling and need comfort.

Prayer: Lord I thank you for the comfort that I receive from the Holy Spirit in every situation. I ask you to help me to be a comforter and blessing to those in need today. Amen.

July 24

Matthew 24:35 "Heaven and earth will pass away, but my words will never pass away." NIV

This earth as we know it and everything around us has a limited life span.

But the Word of the Lord will always stand regardless of all the temporary things around us.

We ought to receive God's Word and hear what He says because it is more dependable than anything we can possibly see around us.

Prayer: Father I thank you for your word that does not pass away. No matter what I see or what things look like I will trust in you and what you have spoken. I thank you for your word that gives me courage today and I praise you for your unchanging word. Amen.

July 25

Psalms 91:4 "He will cover you with his feathers, and under his wings you will find refuge; his faithfulness will be your shield and rampart." NIV

> He promises us to be a complete cover and hide us as a bird covers and protects its little ones from all adversities.
>
> We will find refuge under His wings - the wings of the Almighty.
>
> He is faithful and He is a shield about us today regardless of what we go through.

Prayer: Father I thank you that you are my shield and that I can be completely comforted as you cover me with your wings. I receive it today and enjoy the comfort and peace of being under your wings. Amen.

July 26

Isaiah 26:3 "You will keep in perfect peace those whose minds are steadfast, because they trust in you." NIV

>Peace is not easily bought, sold or found in this natural world - many people seek peace in any way, shape or form.

>But God's peace is perfect!

>When we direct our thoughts, lives and hearts to Him we can enjoy His full peace because we can trust in Him.

Prayer: Lord I thank you for your peace that does surpass all understanding and compares to nothing in this world. I put my heart and thoughts on you today so that I can enjoy your peace. Amen.

July 27

Philippians 4:6 "Do not be anxious about anything, but in every situation, by prayer and petition, with thanksgiving, present your requests to God." NIV

> Not being anxious is a challenge but where anxiety is, faith is absent.
>
> In every situation we need to petition and pray to the Lord with a thanks giving heart.
>
> If we are thankful we overcome our fear and anxiety and we will be reminded what God has already done. Then we can present our requests to God with faith.

Prayer: Lord I thank you that by your grace I will not be anxious or concerned about anything I am facing today, but consistently make my requests known to you with prayer and thanksgiving. Amen.

July 28

Colossians 1:13-14 "For he has rescued us from the dominion of darkness and brought us into the kingdom of the Son he loves, in whom we have redemption, the forgiveness of sins." NIV

> We are rescued - the darkness of this world has no control or hold over us.
>
> We are brought into the kingdom of our Lord Jesus and we belong to Him. We have redemption!
>
> We enjoy complete forgiveness of all our sins because of the completed work of Jesus.

Prayer: Lord I thank you for your goodness that you have rescued me from darkness and from sin. I can walk in your kingdom by your grace. I confess that I am nothing without you and it is all by your strength. I praise you for it today, Amen.

July 29

2 Corinthians 3:18 "And we all, who with unveiled faces contemplate the Lord's glory, are being transformed into his image with ever-increasing glory, which comes from the Lord, who is the Spirit." NIV

Unlike Moses who had to cover his eyes because the glory of the Lord was hurting them, we reflect God's glory every day.

There is a transformation that takes place as we walk with Him every day, being changed into His very image. Even though we are born again it is a constant process to be transformed.

We are becoming like Him with an increasing glory on us which is from the Lord alone. That is what people should be seeing.

Prayer: Lord help me to walk with you every day in truth and sincerity that I can reflect your glory in my very being and lifestyle. I declare my love for you today and commit myself to you. Strengthen me in my walk with you I pray in Jesus' name. Amen.

July 30

2 Corinthians 3:18 "And we all, who with unveiled faces contemplate the Lord's glory, are being transformed into his image with ever-increasing glory, which comes from the Lord, who is the Spirit." NIV

Unlike Moses who had to cover his eyes because the glory of the Lord was hurting them, we reflect God's glory every day.

There is a transformation that takes place as we walk with Him every day, being changed into His very image. Even though we are born again it is a constant process to be transformed.

We are becoming like Him with an increasing glory on us which is from the Lord alone. That is what people should be seeing.

Prayer: Lord help me to walk with you every day in truth and sincerity that I can reflect your glory in my very being and lifestyle. I declare my love for you today and commit myself to you. Strengthen me in my walk with you I pray in Jesus' name. Amen.

July 31

1 Peter 4:1 "Therefore, since Christ suffered in his body, arm yourselves also with the same attitude, because whoever suffers in the body is done with sin. As a result, they do not live the rest of their earthly lives for evil human desires, but rather for the will of God." NIV

Arming ourselves with that same attitude that Christ had with the suffering in our body means to be willing to pay any price in our natural man to prevent sin having a hold on us.

The result is that we don't live, once we have committed ourselves, the life of worldly desires and let it rule our lives.

Because we have put sin to death in our lives we live completely and solely for the will of God - whatever God wants.

Prayer: Lord I willingly lay my life down for you today because I love you. Thank you for the sacrifice you have made for me of suffering to free me from sin. I choose now to do your will and live for you. You are my heart's desire and nothing else matters to me. I praise you. Amen.

August 1

Romans 12:11 "Never be lacking in zeal, but keep your spiritual fervor, serving the Lord." NIV

It is a deliberate decision to maintain zeal and to keep our excitement for the Lord.

It is easy to be distracted and lose our excitement in seeking and enjoying a relationship with Him.

Serving the Lord needs to be our heart's desire and our main focus so we should make every effort to maintain that by exposing ourselves to every anointing we can.

Prayer: Lord I thank you for your love for me and I ask you to cause your Holy Spirit to keep the fire and the zeal going in my heart, to serve you. I acknowledge that without you I am nothing. Amen.

August 2

Psalms 25:20 "Guard my life and rescue me; do not let me be put to shame, for I take refuge in you." NIV

We seek God's protection and help daily as we walk in this world.

It is not God's plan for us to fall or be put to shame in any way. The only protection or guarantee we have is in Him.

Our refuge is only taken in Him and not man or even in the most powerful man/woman of God - the Lord is the only true refuge.

Prayer: I praise you today Lord that you are my rescue and my God and that you will watch over me that there will be no failure or embarrassment. I purposefully take refuge in you and you alone. Amen.

August 3

Ephesians 4:32 "Be kind and compassionate to one another, forgiving each other, just as in Christ God forgave you." NIV

>Our relationship with others is as important as loving God.

>Kindness is doing for others without any reason. Compassion is to be merciful or understanding when people are suffering.

>Forgiveness of each is other is of paramount importance and it should be a constant practice in our everyday lives.

Prayer: Father I thank you for the kindness, love and compassion you have shown me. Help me to express the same to others every day and to forgive people from heart. For I am weak and I look to you to enable me to do your will. I praise you today for all you have done for me. Amen.

August 4

1 John 4:7 "Dear friends, let us love one another, for love comes from God. Everyone who loves has been born of God and knows God." NIV

There is no genuine love outside of God as He alone is love.

Loving each other often causes us to have to deny ourselves and die to our own flesh - it is a decision of the heart.

Loving others is evidence of God being in our lives because without God we cannot love and there is no love outside of God.

Prayer: Lord I praise you for your amazing and unchanging love. Fill me with your love today and help me to receive it and help me to love others unconditionally. Amen.

August 5

Luke 11:9-10 "So I say to you: Ask and it will be given to you; seek and you will find; knock and the door will be opened to you. For everyone who asks receives; the one who seeks finds; and to the one who knocks, the door will be opened." NIV

> We must in fact ask - often we don't have because we fail to ask.
>
> Everyone who asks receives - that is the promise of the Lord. There is no exception or conditions - so go ahead and ask the Lord today!
>
> If we do not make an effort to actually knock or try a door or a situation, it cannot be opened. So us let us not fail in making an effort to ask/knock with an expectancy of God answering us.

Prayer: Lord I praise you today that you are one that answers prayer and you always hear our cry. Today I ask that you take care of what I need and desire. I praise you for it. I thank you as I knock on these doors, I know you will answer it. Amen.

August 6

Philippians 4:13 "I can do all this through him who gives me strength." NIV

It is no shame to acknowledge weakness or struggle to certain things. Half the battle is won by recognizing our limitations.

The Lord strengthens us to do absolutely anything that pertains to His will - "I can do everything".

It is through Christ - there is no strength on this level absent from Jesus.

Prayer: Lord I thank you today that I can be bold and confident to do things I thought I couldn't do because you promised that I can do all things through you. I thank you for strengthening me when I am weak. Amen.

August 7

Ephesians 6:17 "Take the helmet of salvation and the sword of the Spirit, which is the word of God." NIV

The helmet covers the head which symbolizes our thoughts - our minds are renewed with this ongoing salvation we experience and with it we must protect our thoughts.

The sword (which is double edged) is the Word of God - we need God's word to combat the enemy.

Putting on the armor of God in our thought life and knowing God's word helps us to resist and overcome the enemy.

Prayer: Lord I praise you for your salvation and that the word of your testimony and the blood of the lamb will overcome the enemy. Give me the courage today to put on the armor of God and not to cower when the enemy comes against me. Amen.

August 8

Ephesians 6:18 "And pray in the Spirit on all occasions with all kinds of prayers and requests. With this in mind, be alert and always keep on praying for all the Lord's people." NIV

Praying in the Spirit is as Jesus prayed - motivated function and strengthened by God He had the ability to pray long periods because most of our strength originates from our prayer time. Praying in the spirit is essential!

On every occasion we should make prayer our lifestyle and approach in everything we do. We should include the Lord in everything by talking to Him even in public settings.

Staying alert means to be awake spiritually, watching for the enemy and persisting in our prayers means to not give up because God does answer.

Prayer: Lord I thank you that you have answered so many of my prayers and that I have seen the evidence of your faithfulness. Help me to stay diligent with my prayer life. Amen.

August 9

Psalms 18:32-33 "God arms me with strength, and he makes my way perfect. He makes me as surefooted as a deer, enabling me to stand on mountain heights." NLT

God is the one who strengthens us but also makes the way perfect, even though it make look strange to us. The way He makes for us is perfect and beyond our understanding.

The Lord makes us surefooted -which means to be steady and confident in strange places like a deer or goat up in the mountain. They are surefooted and not full of fear.

He enables us to do things like standing on mountain heights. God is our strength and enabler.

Prayer: Lord is upon you this day that I depend and look for strengthening. I pray that you guide me by your spirit and that I will know exactly the path you have laid before me. Amen.

August 10

1 Corinthians 10:13 "The temptations in your life are no different from what others experience. And God is faithful. He will not allow the temptation to be more than you can stand. When you are tempted, he will show you a way out so that you can endure." NLT

> Temptations are reality for all of us. We have different weaknesses and temptations but they are still real for each of us.
>
> God is faithful - we can lean and trust upon Him even when we are struggling with temptation.
>
> He promises that He will not allow temptation too hard for us to bare or that there is no way out - there is a way and we ought to pursue it.

Prayer: Father I thank you that you strengthen me and give me a way out when temptation or the enemy tries to divert me. I thank you for your Holy Spirit that will endure with me to continue to walk in your way and avoid temptations. Thank you for giving me a way out. Amen.

August 11

Nehemiah 8:10 "And Nehemiah continued, "Go and celebrate with a feast of rich foods and sweet drinks, and share gifts of food with people who have nothing prepared. This is a sacred day before our Lord. Don't be dejected and sad, for the joy of the Lord is your strength!" NLT

> This is the day the Lord has made for us and we should not be downcast or miserable.
>
> What gives us strength is His joy, which comes directly from Him as we abide in Him.
>
> So it is time to celebrate for every day God has made new and to enjoy things that we associate with celebration.

Prayer: Lord I celebrate today in your salvation and your greatness that you have made a way and that this is your day. No matter what things look like or what is ahead of me, I will celebrate because your joy is my strength. Amen.

August 12

Romans 7:6 "But now we have been released from the law, for we died to it and are no longer captive to its power. Now we can serve God, not in the old way of obeying the letter of the law, but in the new way of living in the Spirit." NIV

A new way - when Christ came He made all things new and introduced a tremendous kingdom and new salvation.

It is not by trying to observe legalities and fine line tuning of information but rather being led by the Spirit of God's love and way.

Living in the Spirit is total dedication to the Lord and commitment, allowing Him to lead us sincerely - the law of the spirit is greater as it is a much higher standard.

Prayer: Lord help me to be led by the Spirit, to live and walk in the Spirit so that I may do everything that is pleasing in your sight. I acknowledge that I am weak, but I know you are strong so I trust in you and the Holy Spirit to strengthen me. Amen.

August 13

Colossians 3:16 "Let the message about Christ, in all its richness, fill your lives. Teach and counsel each other with all the wisdom he gives. Sing psalms and hymns and spiritual songs to God with thankful hearts." NLT

We must make it a habit to be full of joy and sing songs as an act of praise to Him continually.

We encourage one another with what He has to taught us in the ways of the Lord that we continue in the strength in the Lord.

And we ought to have thankful hearts regardless of how things seem to us in our natural minds. We put these things to practice and watch how the Lord lifts our spirits and those around us. We are sent by God to influence those that He has assigned to us in our lives.

Prayer: Lord help me to be that shining light today and be effective with my worship and my attitude of praise to you regardless of how things seem because my hope comes from you. Amen.

August 14

Hebrews 9:14 "How much more, then, will the blood of Christ, who through the eternal Spirit offered himself unblemished to God, cleanse our consciences from acts that lead to death, so that we may serve the living God!" NIV

Purest blood (unblemished) - the blood of Jesus - with great power to cleanse us of all sins and inequities, shame and guilt.

Conscience is clear - we have nothing to feel guilty or shameful about once that blood has cleansed us as we turn to Him for salvation.

We left death behind and embraced the life of God. We must serve Him which means not only do all that He asks, but to focus our entire being on Him.

Prayer: Lord I praise you for the blood of Jesus that is so powerful and cleanses me of every sin so that I have no shame or guilt. I can rejoice in my salvation no matter what the enemy does to accuse me. Amen.

August 15

Malachi 3:16 "Then those who feared the Lord talked with each other, and the Lord listened and heard. A scroll of remembrance was written in his presence concerning those who feared the Lord and honored his name." NIV

> Fearing the Lord - is to regard, respect, honor and put Him first in every way.
>
> The Lord listens to our conversations and we ought to be aware of that in everything we do and say.
>
> He records everything we do and say in His book of remembrance and therefore we should be mindful what we want recorded.

Prayer: Lord I thank you that you are always attentive to me and that your spirit helps me to regulate the things that I do and say. Help me that the things that are recorded in remembrance is always pleasing to you and of great value. I dedicate my life to you and ask you to have your way with me. Amen.

August 16

1 Peter 5:8-9 "Be alert and of sober mind. Your enemy the devil prowls around like a roaring lion looking for someone to devour. Resist him, standing firm in the faith, because you know that the family of believers throughout the world is undergoing the same kind of sufferings." NIV

We are to be sober - not oblivious or ignorant but be awake and attentive, watching for the enemy who is definitely out to harm us and deter us from our love and relationship with the Lord.

Resisting the devil is to not give in or be intimidated by him for he is overcome. He is more a noise than any threat of destruction.

Being steadfast in our faith means not to waiver in unbelief and to have confidence today that God is our helper.

Prayer: Lord, by your grace, I thank you that you give me the ability to be sober and watchful today and not allowing the enemy to succeed in his attacks or plans against me. I praise you that you are my shield and strength. Amen.

August 17

1 Kings 8:60-61 "so that all the peoples of the earth may know that the Lord is God and that there is no other. And may your hearts be fully committed to the Lord our God, to live by his decrees and obey his commands, as at this time." NIV

>The world is watching us who claim to be His children and they expect us to behave in a certain way that is becoming of representatives of Christ.

>It is His heart that people recognize and are drawn to God because of us in every way.

>Our hearts should be completely His and He will help us in our own lack of strengths, that His glory may be seen through us.

Prayer: Lord help me to be your testimony witness to all people where ever I go. I am weak but I know you are strong in my weakness and I really desire to reflect you as you are my Lord. Amen.

August 18

1 Corinthians 16:2 "On the first day of every week, each one of you should set aside a sum of money in keeping with your income, saving it up, so that when I come no collections will have to be made." NIV

The principle taught here is an attitude of heart and dedication with our finances.

Saving and giving should be a regular thing, as Paul recommends the first day of each week, in relation to how God has blessed us.

If we are in a habit of doing these things then there is no pressure when the time comes to really give as a body to those in need.

Prayer: Lord help me to be a giver with all that you have trusted me with and not to stumble over giving, but be a generous giver that is pleasing in your sight. Thank you for all that you have given me and that I am able to give. Help me to be a joyous giver. Amen.

August 19

Hebrews 6:12 "We do not want you to become lazy, but to imitate those who through faith and patience inherit what has been promised." NIV

It is easy to become lethargic or lose the same zeal we first started with in our walk with the Lord - let us prevent that.

We imitate or follow the examples of those who have gone before us through out the word of God and even people that we know who have dedicated and sacrificed their lives to and for the Lord.

It is through faith and patience that we receive the inheritance waiting for us and all His promises that are "yes" and "amen".

Prayer: Lord help me to continue and persevere today and not become slow or lose heart but to keep with the same diligence and zeal that I began with. Help me Lord for I am weak but I praise you that you are my strength today. Amen.

August 20

Luke 10:19 "I have given you authority to trample on snakes and scorpions and to overcome all the power of the enemy; nothing will harm you." NIV

> Jesus gave us authority over the enemy and onslaughts the enemy might send us - true authority.
>
> To have power over the enemy is something we have to grasp in our hearts so that we have faith because the enemy knows whether we believe or not.
>
> The promise from the Lord is that nothing can hurt us - a true promise from the Lord that we can depend upon.

Prayer: Lord I thank you for the completed work at calvary and by your grace I step into that authority today and I will take charge over anything the enemy tries to do against me, my family and those around me. Lead me by your spirit today to be effective. Amen.

August 21

Philippians 2:1-2 "Therefore if you have any encouragement from being united with Christ, if any comfort from his love, if any common sharing in the Spirit, if any tenderness and compassion, then make my joy complete by being like-minded, having the same love, being one in spirit and of one mind." NIV

We were called to a different life and kingdom to that which the world presents - life with love and fellowship with the Holy Spirit.

We are to be united and like-minded as children of God, having the same spirit as Christ.

The world will know we are His when we are united and live and reflect the nature of Christ.

Prayer: Lord I thank you that you fill me with your purpose and spirit today. Help me to be united with my brethren and to walk in the power of your spirit. I praise you with all my heart because there is no one like you. Amen.

August 22

Matthew 5:6 "Blessed are those who hunger and thirst for righteousness, for they will be filled." NIV

It is good for us to be longing and have a hunger and thirst to be in right standing with our Lord.

Jesus is our righteousness and our covering but to walk with Him in relationship produces right standing.

We are blessed and shall be blessed when we long for this because then we will not only be in relationship with Him, but be covered in His righteousness.

Prayer: Lord, I do hunger and thirst for you and to walk with you. I love you and cannot live without you, you are everything I need. Thank you for your righteousness today. Amen.

August 23

Psalms 37:3 "Trust in the Lord and do good; dwell in the land and feed on His faithfulness." NKJV

Trusting Him means not knowing what's up ahead. If we knew all that God had planned, we wouldn't need to trust Him.

Doing good is to do what is right and pleasing in His sight even when it is not convenient.

Feeding on His faithfulness is to always remember that God never changes no matter what our circumstances look like.

Prayer: Lord I praise you that your hand is upon my life. I ask you to lead me to be an influence and blessing to other people and always bring glory to your name. Amen.

August 24

Psalms 107:9 "For He satisfies the longing soul, And fills the hungry soul with goodness." NKJV

>It is a godly thing to long for the Lord or to have a hunger for Him and His righteousness.
>
>It is to our benefit to always be longing to be with Him, to fellowship with Him and to love Him more than life itself.
>
>We will be satisfied and our hearts will be filled with all that is good when we focus and long for Him.

Prayer: Lord, without you I am nothing and I look to you and praise you for your amazing salvation. Fill my heart with your love and your Holy Spirit today. Thank you that I can enjoy your presence and goodness today. Amen.

August 25

1 Peter 3:12 "For the eyes of the Lord are on the righteous and his ears are attentive to their prayer, but the face of the Lord is against those who do evil." NIV

The Lord is constantly watching -
nothing misses the Lord's attention.

When we choose to do right and make
an effort to do it, we can be assured that
He is even more attentive to our prayers.

The Lord is resistant those who
purposefully do evil and we could and
should pray for mercy for them too.

Prayer: Father I thank you that you hear my prayers and I ask you to help me continually to do what is right in your sight. Help me to have mercy and pray for those that are doing evil that they may be turned towards you. Amen.

August 26

Philippians 1:6 "And I am certain that God, who began the good work within you, will continue his work until it is finally finished on the day when Christ Jesus returns." NLT

When we embark on the journey of salvation with the Lord He begins a work in us.

He continually works on us with a goal and purpose, as much as we allow Him to work in us - we are training for reigning with Him in eternity.

The goal, or the finality, is when the Lord returns to come and get us. We translate from this life into the next. Then there is no more changing or working towards the goal the Lord has planned for us.

Prayer: Father in heaven I thank you that you have begun a good work in me. Help me to surrender to the working and dealing of your hand that I can become all that you want me to be for only there is true contentment found. I praise you today for your patience and kindness with me. Amen.

August 27

Mark 11:24 "I tell you, you can pray for anything, and if you believe that you've received it, it will be yours." NLT

> An unconditional promise - let us take it seriously from the heart and mouth of our Lord Jesus.
>
> Anything means anything - We can ask anything. There is no limit to what we can ask for for what He has promised us.
>
> Jesus did say if you can believe; our faith is under constant attack to deter that very status that we can believe for anything.

Prayer: Lord, teach me to resist and eradicate all unbelief in my life and continually strengthen my faith that I can believe for anything for myself and those around me. Use me today for your glory. Amen.

August 28

Psalms 103:2-4 "Let all that I am praise the Lord; may I never forget the good things he does for me. He forgives all my sins and heals all my diseases. He redeems me from death and crowns me with love and tender mercies." NLT

We ought to remember all that the Lord has done - so often we are only aware of what we don't have instead of what we do have.

The Lord has done so much for us already and if we start looking at those things instead of the things we think we need today, it will cause us to praise and sing.

He has forgiven us of all our sins and He has shown us great mercy through the completed work of Jesus.

Prayer: Lord I praise you today and thank you for the many things you have done for me, my family and those around me. You have been absolutely marvelous and my heart rejoices in you. Today I will not focus on my need or my concerns but rather on the wonderful things you have already done. I praise you. Amen.

August 29

Ephesians 3:20 "Now all glory to God, who is able, through his mighty power at work within us, to accomplish infinitely more than we might ask or think." NLT

> God is able to do anything!
>
> He works within us and around us and does so much for us.
>
> He can do even more than we can ask or think - we cannot even contemplate what God is able to do for us when we ask.

Prayer: Lord I praise you for your great power. You can go even beyond all the things I can imagine and I trust you for all the things I have asked and prayed for today. Lead me by your spirit to be a blessing and to bring life to others so that I may glorify you. Amen.

August 30

Romans 14:17 "For the kingdom of God is not a matter of eating and drinking, but of righteousness, peace and joy in the Holy Spirit," NIV

> God's kingdom is that which He rules over and we belong to it when we accept Him as our savior.
>
> The kingdom of God is different than the world and doesn't consist of these natural things but rather the spiritual things.
>
> We have righteousness, peace and joy - all in the Holy Spirit! We need the Holy Spirit every day and we live and walk in the spirit of God.

Prayer: Lord I praise you today for your salvation and that I am part of your kingdom. I thank you for the great work you have done in me. Help me to walk in the spirit and enjoy the righteousness, peace and joy that you have given me through salvation and spirit. Help me to be a light that the world may say you in me. Amen.

August 31

Hebrews 13:6 "So we say with confidence, "The Lord is my helper; I will not be afraid. What can mere mortals do to me?" NIV

> Because of what the Lord has done we can be bold and full of confidence.
>
> We will not be afraid as the enemy tries to intimidate us with fear for we can be sure that God is definitely going to help us.
>
> People can not do anything to us, no government or anything of this world. Our help is from the Lord.

Prayer: Mighty God I praise you today that you are sovereign and mightier than any government or situation I am facing. I praise you that no one can do me any harm because I have you as a helper and protector. Thank you that you will help me today and in my future. Amen.

September 1

Matthew 5:24 "leave your gift there in front of the altar. First go and be reconciled to them; then come and offer your gift." NIV

> Being reconciled with one another is of utmost importance to the Lord. Even more than anything we can bring Him in sacrifice.
>
> Forgiveness is the very hinge of salvation and we ought to practice forgiveness continually to everyone around us.
>
> What we bring the Lord in service or sacrifice has no value if we are not reconciled.

Prayer: Lord help me today to forgive everyone who has offended me completely from my heart and to be reconciled where possible to those I ought to be. Lead me by your spirit to that exact thing. I need your help in doing this. Amen.

September 2

Romans 14:8 "If we live, we live for the Lord; and if we die, we die for the Lord. So, whether we live or die, we belong to the Lord." NIV

Sometimes we are so anxious about life and/or death but it is all in the hands of God and also just temporary. (except eternal life)

So whatever happens to us or whatever we do do it for the Lord and if He is our goal in all we do we need not be anxious for anything.

We belong to the Lord - we are His property and glad to be such.

Prayer: Lord I praise you today that I have no concern about tomorrow whether I live or die because it is all to you. You are first and foremost in my heart and I declare my love for you today. Amen.

September 3

Psalms 91:9-11 "If you say, "The Lord is my refuge," and you make the Most High your dwelling, no harm will overtake you, no disaster will come near your tent. For he will command his angels concerning you to guard you in all your ways;" NIV

> It is our own decision to give the Lord that place - the Lord's sovereignty and leadership comes first in our lives.
>
> With the promise of doing that we know we can take refuge in Him and no disaster will befall us, our homes or those around us.
>
> God promises us the support of His angelic beings in our lives and our walk if we make Him Lord of everything.

Prayer: Lord today I submit my heart and soul completely to you and thank you that you will lead me and guide me in the way that you want me to be. I choose you in every way and every part of my life. You are Lord of my life. I love you Lord. Amen.

September 4

James 4:7-8 "Submit yourselves, then, to God. Resist the devil, and he will flee from you. Come near to God and he will come near to you. Wash your hands, you sinners, and purify your hearts, you double-minded." NIV

When we submit ourselves to God there is no resistance in our heart to anything that He desires from us, even if we don't always understand what it is He wants.

Only once we are submitted are we able to resist the enemy and all that he tries to do. And the promise is that the enemy will absolutely run from us.

In our effort to draw near to Him we are very confident that He will draw near to us because of His promise to do so.

Prayer: How I praise you this day Lord for your great love and kindness toward me! Teach me to continually submit to you in every way and to resist the enemy, that he will have no hold on me or my household. In Jesus name. Amen.

September 5

1 Peter 2:9 "But you are a chosen people, a royal priesthood, a holy nation, God's special possession, that you may declare the praises of him who called you out of darkness into his wonderful light." NIV

> Declaring the praises of God - it is our privilege and duty to continually declare His praises, to praise Him and to let others see us always praising our Lord.
>
> He chose us and made us His chosen people - how blessed we are that He did so!
>
> We are called out of the darkness into His wonderful light and what a great privilege it is. We praise Him today for all He has done.

Prayer: Lord I praise you and thank you for choosing me and saving me. I ask you to fill me with your spirit and joy today. I declare your praises every moment and with every opportunity I have so that you may be glorified through my talk and my life. Amen.

September 6

Philippians 4:11 "I am not saying this because I am in need, for I have learned to be content whatever the circumstances." NIV

Paul said he learned to be content - it did not come naturally - it is a process over a period of time to find contentment in the Lord rather than our circumstances.

Whether we be in need or not it should not influence our state of joy or contentment. Any difficulty should not steal our joy because we find happiness in the consistency of our Lord and His goodness.

Whatever the circumstances - this does not come naturally or quickly but over life's journey we learn that we do not rise and fall because of circumstances but by the grace of God.

Prayer: Lord I praise you for your wonderful salvation and that I can find joy and contentment in you no matter what difficulty I face today. Help me to continually to learn to be content and I pray that you fill me with your joy and that no difficulty I face will steal that joy. Amen.

September 7

3 John 1:2 "Dear friend, I pray that you may enjoy good health and that all may go well with you, even as your soul is getting along well." NIV

It is God's pleasure that we enjoy the quality of life on earth, good health and all that we need. We can believe for that.

Go well with you - to go well with us is not only joy and contentment, but also God's pleasure that we have lack in nothing.

As our soul is getting along well - our soul is where our will, thoughts and passions all lay - submitted to the Lord the soul prospers as we grow in the Lord and causes all things in the natural around us to prosper.

Prayer: Lord I praise you today and thank you for your salvation. I thank you that my soul prospers and grow in you daily because of your goodness and that you will cause me to have all that I need and walk in health. Amen.

September 8

Philippians 4:6 "Do not be anxious about anything, but in every situation, by prayer and petition, with thanksgiving, present your requests to God." NIV

Not to be anxious! It is an ongoing effort not to become anxious or reactionary to a situation or challenge we might have. We "have" to practice not becoming anxious.

By praying and laying our requests before the Lord with a thankful heart we can make whatever situation known to Him.

We can request anything to the Lord with confidence that He will hear and answer and we ought to be satisfied with whatever answer He gives us.

Prayer: Lord I thank you and praise you today that you hear my prayers. Help me and teach me your ways to not be anxious or reactionary. I falter so many times in a panic and so I ask you to help me today to see in whom my strength lay. Amen.

September 9

John 10:10 "The thief's purpose is to steal and kill and destroy. My purpose is to give them a rich and satisfying life." NLT

> The enemy is real and his goal is to kill, steal and destroy but Jesus came to give us life.
>
> His purpose is to give us a rich and satisfying life - the fullness and all things complete.
>
> Jesus paid a very dear price that we can have this completeness. Let's take all we can from this.

Prayer: Lord I praise you for your salvation and that you died for me and that you gave me this amazing life. I will follow you and expect to have a life that is rich and full in you. Amen.

September 10

Psalms 37:23 "The Lord directs the steps of the godly. He delights in every detail of their lives." NLT

> God "organizes" our direction and the way we are going. He makes sure we are going in the right direction.
>
> He is involved in every detail of our lives with great excitement - we are that important to Him!
>
> We are the apple of His eye and God is thoroughly involved in us when we pursue and seek Him in every part of our lives.

Prayer: Lord I thank you that you direct my path and that you are my helper. I praise you that you will always cause me to go the way you want me to go. I trust in you today that you will help me make every right decision according to your will. Amen.

September 11

1 John 4:16 "And so we know and rely on the love God has for us. God is love. Whoever lives in love lives in God, and God in them." NIV

> We do not need to rely on our efforts or our works but we can depend and rely on His love for us.

> There is no love outside of God - All true love has its origin in Him.

> If we live, behave, eat and breathe love, God lives in us.

Prayer: Lord I thank you for your love for me and that I can rely on it. Fill me with your love continually so that I will express your love naturally to all those around me and to you. I choose to love you with all my heart today. Amen.

September 12

Romans 13:9-10 ""Love your neighbor as yourself." Love does no harm to a neighbor. Therefore love is the fulfillment of the law." NIV

> The perfect law is to do to others as you want them to do to you, and in that way fulfill the complete law.
>
> When we walk and live in love we won't harm our neighbor or anyone around us. It is natural and automatic.
>
> If we function this way there would be so much love and harmony all around us. Our families, our churches, at work and our environment.

Prayer: Lord, fill me with this love because I cannot do it by myself. I need you Lord and your love to dwell inside me on a continual basis that I can love this way. Amen.

September 13

Hebrews 6:11-12 "We want each of you to show this same diligence to the very end, so that what you hope for may be fully realized. We do not want you to become lazy, but to imitate those who through faith and patience inherit what has been promised." NIV

Showing diligence is to not give up even when we lose heart or become tired.

It is possible for us to become lazy or lethargic in our journey to complete the race God has given us, each individually.

We are to take our example from those throughout history who walked with the Lord., who through faith and patience, have inherited their promises from God.

Prayer: Lord I pray that you will help me to not get tired or give up today with the things you have promised me . Help me to endure and to continually pursue by faith, the things you have called me to do Lord. Amen.

September 14

Joshua 24:15 "But as for me and my household, we will serve the Lord." NIV

Serving God is a decision and a definite act of our will and may cost us friends, family and even our jobs at times.

We set the example and tone for our family to put God first, to serve Him and to give Him all the honor in every way.

Serving God with all our hearts is putting Him first - loving the Lord even if we are the only ones in our working environment, school environment or anywhere we find ourselves. Serving God will reap dividends.

Prayer: Lord, my household and I do choose to serve you and to put you first in everything. I choose that even when others around me stop serving you I will not. I will serve you with all my heart today and forever. Amen.

September 15

Ecclesiastes 11:1 "Throw your bread upon the waters, for you will find it after many days." NLV

>Often when we sow and do things it seems to take so long to see the results or that we so hope for.
>
>After "many days" it will come back to you. It will find its way - we have to be patient even though it might take very long.
>
>The delay or time we wait should not deter us in "casting our bread on the waters" or sowing or doing that which is right even if it takes long to be rewarded.

Prayer: Lord I do cast my bread upon the water today and I do sow my seeds and I will make an effort to do what is right in your sight even if it may take a long time for me to see the benefits of it. I choose you and your ways today. Amen.

September 16

Titus 2:11 "For the grace of God has appeared that offers salvation to all people. It teaches us to say "No" to ungodliness and worldly passions, and to live self-controlled, upright and godly lives in this present age," NIV

> The grace - the underserved favor of God - is an immense gift from God to all of us and brings us underserving salvation.
>
> No one is excluded from this grace.
>
> It also teaches us to choose godly ways - the same grace that saves us gives us the ability and desire to live right.

Prayer: Lord I give you thanks for this immense grace and I receive it with all my heart. I thank you for the same grace that helps me and me teaches me to do what is right in your sight that I may please you at all times with my choices, attitude and heart. I love you Lord and I put you first. Amen.

September 17

Luke 9:23 "Then he said to them all: "Whoever wants to be my disciple must deny themselves and take up their cross daily and follow me." NIV

> If we choose the Lord there is a price to pay - total self denial.
>
> When we follow Him it is only what He wants and His purpose and desire matters in our lives.
>
> It is a daily decision to follow Him and to surrender all to Him every single day.

Prayer: Lord I thank you for this wonderful salvation that I enjoy every day. I do choose to put you first, to take up my cross and to follow you and deny myself by your grace. You come first Lord in every way today. Amen.

September 18

Psalms 100:4 "Enter his gates with thanksgiving and his courts with praise; give thanks to him and praise his name." NIV

Before we can even enter the outer court we have to enter the gates with thanks - God loves thankfulness.

We ought to make a habit and lifestyle of praise every day as we approach the Lord and His throne of grace.

We learn to give thanks to Him for all that He is and all He has done for us and continually praise Him for it. It brings joy and excitement when praising Him becomes a lifestyle.

Prayer: Lord I praise you today and give you thanks for all that you've done for me and my family. I praise you for you are wonderful and mighty and there is no one like you. Hallelujah! Amen.

September 19

Proverbs 6:10-11 "A little sleep, a little slumber, a little folding of the hands to rest—and poverty will come on you like a thief and scarcity like an armed man." NIV

>Though the Lord doesn't promote dead works He does like us to stay busy and to be faithful with what He has given us to do, and not to be lazy.

>Poverty will come if we don't do our part and work - work is a blessing.

>The Lord set an example of activity and faithfulness to the work and the task set before Him.

Prayer: Lord I embrace and accept my responsibilities in work. I refuse to be lazy and choose to be an example to others in everything I do. All the daily tasks and work I do, I do it unto You today. You are my King and my Lord and I praise you. Amen.

September 20

Ephesians 4:2-3 "Be completely humble and gentle; be patient, bearing with one another in love. Make every effort to keep the unity of the Spirit through the bond of peace." NIV

> Becoming humble and gentle takes genuine effort and relationship with the Lord on a continual daily basis.
>
> To bear one another in love is developing tolerance through the Spirit. If we all do that it would be a very peaceful world.
>
> We need to make an effort to keep the unity of the Spirit - it doesn't just happen, we must work at it.

Prayer: Lord I submit myself to you and to your word. With every desire in my heart I want to humble my heart and work at keeping peace with my brethren and unity of the Spirit. Help me today to have your spirit in my relationships with the family of God. Amen.

September 21

Mark 7:15 "Nothing outside a person can defile them by going into them. Rather, it is what comes out of a person that defiles them." NIV

We are in this world but not of this world and therefore subject to a lot of the conditions around us that we often think make us unclean - but not so.

Uncleanliness comes from what comes out of us - things we say and do, motivations and wrong attitudes.

It takes the grace of God to put a watch in front of our mouths that we do not allow these unclean things to come out of us, that we are clean of heart and motive.

Prayer: Lord renew my heart today I pray that there be nothing come out of my heart that is unclean or evil or detrimental to anyone around me, that I may be a life source for your name's sake. Amen.

September 22

1 John 5:3-4 "In fact, this is love for God: to keep his commands. And his commands are not burdensome, for everyone born of God overcomes the world. This is the victory that has overcome the world, even our faith." NIV

> When we love the Lord it becomes natural for us to keep His commands/teachings.
>
> His ways are not hard or difficult - "His yoke is easy and light"
>
> By faith we walk this way and overcome all that is negative. Our hope and faith is in God. We do not follow in the ways of the world but the ways of God.

Prayer: Lord I love you with all my heart and choose to follow you. I thank you for your grace that gives me the ability to do this and not to succumb or submit to the world but follow you in every way. I choose you today from my heart. Amen.

September 23

Proverbs 18:4 "The words of the mouth are deep waters, but the fountain of wisdom is a rushing stream." NIV

>Words are very powerful and effect and challenge things around us and we ought to allow the Holy Spirit to control the words we speak.
>
>Jesus had the words of life and because we have Him inside of us we ought to allow it to freely come out of us to all those around us.
>
>Wisdom of God flows through our lives and is refreshing like a "bubbling brook".

Prayer: Lord help me to be a bubbling brook today, allowing your words to flow through me with wisdom, kindness and love that I might be a instrument of your words of life today. In Jesus' name, Amen.

September 24

Galatians 3:11 "Clearly no one who relies on the law is justified before God, because "the righteous will live by faith.""" NIV

Justification - to be made righteous and justified by the wonderful completed work of Jesus is a gift from God.

The law didn't justify us or help us but only pointed us towards this amazing salvation and grace of God.

The righteous - those who are in right standing with Him - will live by faith and trust in God.

Prayer: Lord I thank you for this amazing gift of salvation that I am so underserving of. Help me to continue to walk in faith in my salvation and to know that you are my helper. I look to you today to strengthen my faith as I walk in this justification and become sanctified day by day. Amen.

September 25

Acts 20:24 "However, I consider my life worth nothing to me; my only aim is to finish the race and complete the task the Lord Jesus has given me—the task of testifying to the good news of God's grace." NIV

> As we walk with the Lord our lives become less significant on this earth as He increases in importance.
>
> We have a race/task before us that we need to complete.
>
> The task is given by the Lord and each one of us must finish that race He has given us.

Prayer: Lord I praise you today that you have saved me and given me a task and vision to complete. Help me and strengthen me that I can do this task and finish this race exactly as you asked me to. I love you and I put you first today. Amen.

September 26

Mark 11:24 "Therefore I tell you, whatever you ask for in prayer, believe that you have received it, and it will be yours." NIV

> Whatever means we could ask for anything - there is no limit to what we can ask for.
>
> When we pray and we believe what we are asking for it is a sure thing, according to the words of Jesus, and we ought to believe that we already have it.
>
> "and it will be yours" - emphasis is will be -the timing and the way God will do it, is to be seen.

Prayer: Lord I thank you for this wonderful promise that you have given me that I can have anything I ask for and I can believe for. I make my requests known to you with confidence today and I know that I have already received it. I praise you for it! In Jesus' name. Amen.

September 27

Acts 27:25 "So keep up your courage, men, for I have faith in God that it will happen just as he told me." NIV

> We are to keep up our courage no matter what our circumstances look like.
>
> We ought to have faith in God who never fails us - And faith comes from hearing.
>
> Whatever He has told us that, is what we are going to believe and help keep our courage with.

Prayer: Lord I thank you for your word which gives me faith that I can believe even in the midst of my circumstances. I look to and trust in you today. Amen.

September 28

Luke 7:47 "Therefore, I tell you, her many sins have been forgiven—as her great love has shown. But whoever has been forgiven little loves little." NIV

When the Lord forgive sins, He forgives them completely and is irrespective of the volume - one or many makes no difference.

When we understand how much we are forgiven of, we are so grateful and tend to appreciate and love the Lord all the more.

We do not take for granted our complete forgiveness or forget, even after years of serving Him, all our inequity and sin He has taken from us which causes us now to absolutely adore, praise and thank Him.

Prayer: Lord I praise you today from the depth of my heart for the many sins you have forgiven me of - great and small - each and every one of them. I praise you for this wonderful salvation Lord. Thank you. Help me also to forgive others completely as you have forgiven me. Amen.

September 29

Ephesians 6:11 "Put on the full armor of God, so that you can take your stand against the devil's schemes." NIV

> The scheme and the plan of the devil is a very real thing against each of us.
>
> Putting on the entire armor of God, not just part of if, will ensure us a very secure stand against the devil and complete victory.
>
> We must not flee or run from the enemy but make a stand against him - We have full authority.

Prayer: Lord today I put on the whole armor of God and I stand against these attacks/schemes of the enemy. I will not succumb to him and I thank you that you have given me complete authority and victory over him. Thank you for the completed work at calvary. Amen.

September 30

1 Thessalonians 4:11-12 "and to make it your ambition to lead a quiet life: You should mind your own business and work with your hands, just as we told you, so that your daily life may win the respect of outsiders and so that you will not be dependent on anybody." NIV

> We are not to be lazy and work hard, and win the respect of others just by doing so.
>
> And if we make it our goal and ambition to live a non "nosy" life where we mind our own business, it will produce a good testimony around us.
>
> Our daily life and behavior should win the respect and regard of others, giving us a platform to share Christ with them.

Prayer: Lord, by your grace I focus on what you have given me to do and work hard today as unto you. Help me to mind my own business so that I might be a testimony and example to others around me to win them to you. For you name's sake, Amen.

October 1

1 John 5:14-15 "This is the confidence we have in approaching God: that if we ask anything according to his will, he hears us. And if we know that he hears us—whatever we ask—we know that we have what we asked of him." NIV

> Asking according to His will comes from having a relationship with Him - We automatically ask according to His will.
>
> We can be confident that He hears us when we ask and all our petitions are clear to Him.
>
> We have His promise that He not only hears our prayers but answers and does what we ask of Him.

Prayer: Lord I thank you that I pray according to your will and your purpose and that you not only hear them, but answer them. No matter how long it takes or seemingly challenging I know that you'll answer my prayer today. Amen.

October 2

Luke 6:38 "Give, and it will be given to you. A good measure, pressed down, shaken together and running over, will be poured into your lap. For with the measure you use, it will be measured to you." NIV

Giving is a vital part of our christian walk and should be done with excitement and joy.

The promise is of the return of what we give in such a way that it is overflowing in abundance.

The same attitude and sacrifice we use in our giving will be the same way we receive - let us therefor be extremely generous today.

Prayer: Lord I want to be generous just like you are - a joyful and excited giver. Help me to not be attached to things but rather give like you give, today and the rest of my life. Amen.

October 3

Psalms 143:10 "Teach me to do your will, for you are my God; may your good Spirit lead me on level ground." NIV

> Learning to do His will is a process of wanting to know and learn from Him.
>
> We want to do the will of God because it pleases Him and He is our God.
>
> "Lead me in your way Lord I pray " is the prayer of our hearts in His "uprightness".

Prayer: Lord I do choose to follow you today and I ask you to teach me your ways. Lead me in your will only Lord that I can do your will and walk in your uprightness. Amen.

October 4

1 Corinthians 10:13 "No temptation has overtaken you except what is common to mankind. And God is faithful; he will not let you be tempted beyond what you can bear. But when you are tempted, he will also provide a way out so that you can endure it." NIV

> God is in control of what is allowed in our lives - God will not allow us to be tempted beyond what we are able.
>
> God is faithful and we can depend upon Him.
>
> There is always a way out, no matter how hard or difficult it may seem to us. He has already prepared the way out - we ought to always look for the way out when we are in a tempting situation.

Prayer: Lord I dedicate my heart and life to you. Help me to not be weak and give into any temptation, but to always look for the way out that you have provided, that I may walk in ways that is right in your sight. Amen.

October 5

Matthew 6:33 "But seek first his kingdom and his righteousness, and all these things will be given to you as well." NIV

> Putting first things first - God's Kingdom always comes first.
>
> His righteousness which comes as a gift from God, is what we pursue.
>
> We can expect everything else that often seems to be more important to be "added".

Prayer: Lord today I choose to seek your kingdom and be in right standing with you as I walk with you, and that the other things that take my attention will be added or what I need will be supplied. I praise you today for your great salvation. Amen.

October 6

Mark 16:15-16 "He said to them, "Go into all the world and preach the gospel to all creation. Whoever believes and is baptized will be saved, but whoever does not believe will be condemned." NIV

> It is our mandate to carry this gospel and message to everyone.
>
> He who believes will be saved - an amazing promise to all to receive Christ. There is no exception.
>
> Those who do not receive Him as Savior and Lord are already condemned. It is our duty to at least carry this message to them to give them a choice.

Prayer: Lord use me for your witness to carry your name and message to all those in need and do not know the gospel. Help me to be a shining light I pray today. Amen.

October 7

Galatians 2:20 "I have been crucified with Christ and I no longer live, but Christ lives in me. The life I now live in the body, I live by faith in the Son of God, who loved me and gave himself for me." NIV

> The old man is dead and the new man who lives is resurrected with Christ.
>
> And Jesus lives in me and through me every day as I am dead to myself.
>
> Now a new life is founded on faith in Him and confidence in His unchanging love and goodness.

Prayer: Lord I thank you that I am a new creation and that the old man is dead. I thank you that you give me confidence and empower me to live the new life rather than habits from the old.

October 8

1 Timothy 1:18-19 "Timothy, my son, I am giving you this command in keeping with the prophecies once made about you, so that by recalling them you may fight the battle well, holding on to faith and a good conscience, which some have rejected and so have suffered shipwreck with regard to the faith." NIV

> God's directed promises and prophetic words are a source of life and empowerment to fight the good fight.
>
> The good fight is a fight that we are destined to win by faith in Him - a life filled with victories.
>
> Maintaining good conscience at all times and holding on to this faith regardless of what things look like - His promises are yes and amen.

Prayer: Lord I thank you for your word and those that are directed to me personally. Help me to be reminded of them and put my faith and confidence in your promises as you are always faithful. Amen.

October 9

Psalms 16:11 "You make known to me the path of life; you will fill me with joy in your presence, with eternal pleasures at your right hand." NIV

>God shows us the way if we will pay attention.

>Joy is our right, our portion and great reward as we stay in His presence.

>The pleasures the Lord gives us are all without end (eternal). Thanks be to the Lord!

Prayer: Lord I choose to follow you and the path you have laid before me today. Help me to stay focused on your will, love and goodness. Amen.

October 10

James 4:7 "Submit yourselves, then, to God. Resist the devil, and he will flee from you." NIV

Submitting to God means total unquestioning abandonment and trust.

We often confuse agreement with submission - we don't have to be in an agreement, just totally yielded and submitted.

Resisting the devil is not giving in to his temptations, thoughts or attacks but to constantly keep him at bay in our hearts and minds, life and actions.

Prayer: Lord I choose to completely submit to you today and trust you regardless of what I do not understand or try to understand. I submit to you and resist the enemy, knowing that he will flee from me. Amen.

October 11

Hebrews 4:16 "Let us then approach God's throne of grace with confidence, so that we may receive mercy and find grace to help us in our time of need." NIV

> Because of the finished work of Jesus the veil was torn and we can approach the Holy of Holies with boldness.
>
> The throne that God sits on is full of abounding grace and we can receive mercy.
>
> We can receive mercy in our time of need - we are undeserving but because of God's great grace we can expect Him to help us.

Prayer: Lord I do approach your throne with boldness and confidence because of the completed work of our Lord Jesus. And I come to you today with my requests and make it known to you, expecting you to hear and answer. Amen.

October 12

Jude 1:24 "To him who is able to keep you from stumbling and to present you before his glorious presence without fault and with great joy" NIV

> God is able to keep us from falling at all times.
>
> Our Lord Jesus presents us to the Father, redeemed and righteous - because He is our righteousness.
>
> It gives Jesus joy, having had obtained victory on the cross, to present us to the Father.

Prayer: Lord I praise you today for this wonderful salvation, that you are my righteousness and that you are able to keep me from falling till that day. I thank you for your strength. Help me to be your testimony today. Amen.

October 13

Psalms 95:6-7 "Come, let us bow down in worship, let us kneel before the Lord our Maker; for he is our God and we are the people of his pasture, the flock under his care." NIV

Bowing down is an expression of a heartfelt attitude of worship - worshippers are the only thing God is seeking.

He alone is our God - there is no other!

We are His sheep - His own and under His care. We can expect Him to nurture us and watch over us.

Prayer: Lord I thank you that I am yours because of the completed work at calvary. I am so grateful today that I am your child and under your care. Help me to follow you and worship you from the depth of my heart. Amen.

October 14

Romans 8:26 "In the same way, the Spirit helps us in our weakness. We do not know what we ought to pray for, but the Spirit himself intercedes for us through wordless groans." NIV

Jesus asked us to wait for the Holy Spirit because we need Him so much to be effective.

In our lack of ability to pray, the Holy Spirit prays for us, through us and in us - sometimes with strange manifestations.

We can yield to the Holy Spirit's ability to pray through us more often to accomplish God's plan quicker.

Prayer: Lord I yield to your Holy Spirit and I thank you for your Spirit. I ask that you will allow him to pray through me daily your purpose and plans. Help me Holy Spirit, for I am weak and you are strong. Amen.

October 15

Philippians 4:19 "And my God will meet all your needs according to the riches of his glory in Christ Jesus." NIV

There are no exceptions - ALL my needs will be met.

According to His riches, which are abounding and uncountable so we can expect our needs to be met over and above.

God is our provider even when we feel undeserving.

Prayer: Lord I thank you for your provision today and make known to you my needs, expecting you will answer because of your word. Amen.

October 16

Matthew 7:7 "Ask and it will be given to you; seek and you will find; knock and the door will be opened to you. For everyone who asks receives; the one who seeks finds; and to the one who knocks, the door will be opened." NIV

> Often we don't have because we didn't really ask.
>
> Even when we ask sometimes it is almost without expectancy - today it changes. Today we will pray and ask with expectancy.
>
> For everyone who asks, receives - there are no conditions just a promise.

Prayer: Lord I thank you for your promises and your words that are true. I ask today and make my needs known to you because you answer me and I will receive because I ask of you. Hallelujah! Amen.

October 17

Mark 16:15 "He said to them, "Go into all the world and preach the gospel to all creation." NIV

It is every believer's obligation and calling to share the gospel with anyone they possibly can.

When Jesus saved us He automatically called us as disciples to carry out this wonderful good news of salvation to everyone around us.

We also know that some sow, some water and some reap - it must not stop us from sharing when we don't see the results immediately or soon.

Prayer: Lord lead me to be a witness and a disciple of yours to preach that good news to someone today and every day. Give me a soul a day I pray. Amen.

October 18

Exodus 23:25-26 "Worship the Lord your God, and his blessing will be on your food and water. I will take away sickness from among you, and none will miscarry or be barren in your land. I will give you a full life span." NIV

> When God blesses there is nothing that can stop His blessing!
>
> When we serve God (putting Him at the center of our lives) we can expect Him to bless and provide for us and to give us health.
>
> Barrenness, miscarriage and sickness is not to be amongst us - It is our privilege not to have these things.

Prayer: Lord I thank you for your blessings today. I choose to put you at the center of my life and serve you with all of my heart. You are first, second and third in my life and I praise you for all your blessings and kindness towards me. Amen.

October 19

Romans 8:38 "For I am convinced that neither death nor life, neither angels nor demons, neither the present nor the future, nor any powers, neither height nor depth, nor anything else in all creation, will be able to separate us from the love of God that is in Christ Jesus our Lord." NIV

God's love is consistent and unconditional and there is just nothing that can get between His love and us.

We have to be constantly reminded that God loves us without any conditions. The enemy tries to steal that knowledge and reassurance.

The love we receive from God is all because of the completed work of our Lord Jesus at calvary.

Prayer: Lord I praise you for your amazing love that is never ceasing. Fill me with your love that I may receive it, enjoy it and share it every day of my life. I praise you today. Amen.

October 20

1 Timothy 1:7 "For the Spirit God gave us does not make us timid, but gives us power, love and self-discipline." NIV

> Fear is a trap and direct target from the devil. Fear does not come from anywhere else but the devil.
>
> God gave us a spirit of power and love because He is love and it should be evident in our lives - not fear.
>
> A sound mind - so often we feel that we are "losing our mind" but we have a sound mind because of Christ and we should confess it daily.

Prayer: I praise you for my sound mind Lord, and my fearless heart that is full of love. I praise you God that you fill me constantly with this knowledge and this reassurance of your love. I praise your lovely name today. Amen.

October 21

Psalms 27:14 "Wait for the Lord; be strong and take heart and wait for the Lord." NIV

> Waiting is to be directed and dependent upon Him.
>
> Waiting on the Lord is also an expectancy and dependency that God will do something and;
>
> Not getting an immediate answer but being patient until the answer, solution or breakthrough comes.

Prayer: Lord I will wait for you and I know you will strengthen my heart while I wait, for your strength comes to me when I am weak. I give you glory and praise for that today. Amen.

October 22

Isaiah 26:3-4 "You will keep in perfect peace those whose minds are steadfast, because they trust in you. Trust in the Lord forever, for the Lord, the Lord himself, is the Rock eternal." NIV

> The world does not give peace the way God gives peace - without Him there is no peace.
>
> Our mind has to be focused on Him and our thought life completely disciplined and targeted on that of the Lord.
>
> Our trust should be in Him, which means that regardless what we see, feel or how things look, God will come through because of His goodness.

Prayer: Lord I thank you for your peace which surpasses all understanding. I will constantly discipline myself to think only of you and what you say and whichever way your Word directs me because I trust in you. You will not let me down. Amen.

October 23

Isaiah 55:11 "so is my word that goes out from my mouth: It will not return to me empty, but will accomplish what I desire and achieve the purpose for which I sent it." NIV

God's word is all powerful - Jesus used God's word to defeat the devil.

It never returns to God without fruitfulness.

He has given us the command to speak His word, even to the mountain.

Prayer: Lord I thank you for your word that does not return void and that it is powerful to us and through us, for your purposes. Help me to speak your word today and to pray your word that I can be effective and fruitful for you. Amen.

October 24

2 Corinthians 9:7 "Each of you should give what you have decided in your heart to give, not reluctantly or under compulsion, for God loves a cheerful giver." NIV

It is with great excitement that we give to the ones we love, and it is with that same joyfulness that we should give to God because we love Him.

The enemy would like to steal our excitement in giving to God by placing fear in our hearts and confusing our thoughts.

We should purpose in our heart and make it a life style of giving - with excitement - because we know that we love Him and that He returns to us a hundredfold.

Prayer: Lord, help me to be a giver in every way all my life, and to be cheerful and excited as you are glad about giving to me. Help me to be obedient to give what you tell me, not only to the storehouse, but also to those in need around me. Amen.

October 25

Psalms 36:7 "How priceless is your unfailing love! Both high and low among men find refuge in the shadow of your wings." NIV

> There is nothing that can compare to God's love for us - NOTHING can stop Him loving us.
>
> "High and low" among men, means all different kinds of people, take refuge in His love. He loves everyone so dearly.
>
> We should reflect that love that He has, even for the lost and wicked people.

Prayer: Lord I praise you today for this unfailing love throughout my life that I have received and will continue to receive. Fill me with your love, even for the lost and those that do wrong things, that I will love them the way you love them Lord. Amen.

October 26

Galatians 2:20 "I have been crucified with Christ and I no longer live, but Christ lives in me. The life I now live in the body, I live by faith in the Son of God, who loved me and gave himself for me." NIV

> The old man and the old nature is dead with Christ (and it should stay that way).
>
> Now we live in our Lord Jesus and through Him - He gives us strength.
>
> This life that we live is a complete life of faith, that the Lord will glorify Himself through us.

Prayer: Lord I acknowledge today that I am completely yours and that you live through me. Help me to be completely yielded to you today. I love you Lord with all my heart.

October 27

Lamentations 3:22 "Because of the Lord's great love we are not consumed, for his compassions never fail. They are new every morning; great is your faithfulness." NIV

> Each day that is new is a day that the Lord has made and His mercies are new that day.
>
> His faithfulness is not only great, but everlasting and we ought to rejoice in every new day.
>
> The Lord's great love is beyond measure.

Prayer: Lord I rejoice in this day that you have made and receive all your mercies that are new today. I praise you from the bottom of my heart for how great you are today. Amen.

October 28

James 1:17 "Every good and perfect gift is from above, coming down from the Father of the heavenly lights, who does not change like shifting shadows." NIV

> God is the "good" gift giver.
>
> He is the father of light which illuminates all things that are hidden in the darkness that we can walk in the light, truth and complete openness.
>
> He never changes and is always consistent and faithful.

Prayer: Lord I receive all those good gifts that come from you and I rejoice today that I can walk in the light through your mercy and grace. I declare that I am yours completely Lord. Amen.

October 29

1 Chronicles 16:8-9 "Give praise to the Lord, proclaim his name; make known among the nations what he has done. Sing to him, sing praise to him; tell of all his wonderful acts." NIV

It is a life style we develop of thankfulness to give constant thanks to the Lord - there is so much to be grateful for.

We ought to make known to all people what God has done. He deserves all the honor and praise.

Singing to Him in praise and worship is what we were born to do. God is so worthy!

Prayer: Lord today I praise you and sing praise to you from my heart because you have done great things in my life. My hope and my trust is in your faithfulness. Amen.

October 30

1 Corinthians 15:57 "But thanks be to God! He gives us the victory through our Lord Jesus Christ." NIV

We continue to give thanks to God in every circumstance because He does not change.

We can always expect a victory from the Lord no matter what situation we are facing today.

Our victory and breakthrough always comes because of our Lord Jesus - praise be His name!

Prayer: Lord I thank you today that I can expect victory through my Lord Jesus because you are my helper and my friend, my Lord and savior. Amen.

October 31

Luke 1:37 "For nothing is impossible with God." NLT

We must remind ourselves that there are no limits in God even though we see so many limitations around us.

God is the source for the impossible and we should put our faith in motion for the impossible things.

Jesus said these words to his disciples and we should take it personally.

Prayer: Lord I thank you that nothing is impossible for you. No matter what I face or need from you, there are no limits and I can believe you for what seems to be impossible. Amen.

November 1

2 Corinthians 8:9 "For you know the grace of our Lord Jesus Christ, that though he was rich, yet for your sake he became poor, so that you through his poverty might become rich." NIV

Generous grace - grace we not only don't deserve, but it is so much grace that it is overwhelming and we are blessed to be recipients.

He gave up all position of wealth and all He had so that we could have it - we ought to be rich in every way, both the natural and supernatural.

He loves us so much and it would be a waste if we do not participate in all that He suffered so that we could have - it is a great gift.

Prayer: Father I thank you for this amazing grace that you so generously gave to me. Help me to enjoy it and fully benefit from all that you gave up. I give you praise for your great generosity from the depth of my heart. Amen.

November 2

1 Corinthians 13:4 "Love is patient, love is kind. It does not envy, it does not boast, it is not proud." NIV

Patience is also a fruit but it is evidence of real love.

Kindness - doing for others without any reason. When we function in love that is what we do for others without any reason or logic.

When we function and flow in love we will not be envious but rather be glad for others to have anything and everything.

Prayer: Lord fill me with your love that the evidence of your love will be visible fruit in my life that I can be effective in reflecting you in every way. Thank you for your love towards me. Amen.

November 3

2 Corinthians 9:8 "And God will generously provide all you need. Then you will always have everything you need and plenty left over to share with others." NLT

God is the ultimate provider. He provides generously - which means more than we actually need.

He gives us more than we need so that we can share with others and be a blessing. It is something we need to practice and make a habit of in our lives.

The promise is that we will always have plenty.

Prayer: Lord I thank you that you promised that you would generously provide all that I need. I thank you that I don't need to worry or panic today about tomorrow because you will supply all my needs generously. Help me to share with others because you have given me more than I need and I thank you for it. Amen.

November 4

1 Corinthians 15:58 "Therefore, my dear brothers and sisters, stand firm. Let nothing move you. Always give yourselves fully to the work of the Lord, because you know that your labor in the Lord is not in vain." NIV

> We are not to be moved by our circumstances or any challenges we might experience.
>
> It is the will of the Lord for us to be focused on what He has given each one of us specifically to do.
>
> We will reap what we sow in our labors of love for the Lord, so even if we do not see results or feel appreciated, there will be a time of blessing.

Prayer: Lord help me to stay focused on what you have called me to do. Help me to stand firm and not be shaken or moved by any situation that comes my way. Amen.

November 5

1 Corinthians 9:22 "To the weak I became weak, to win the weak. I have become all things to all people so that by all possible means I might save some." NIV

>Not being legalistic or religious, we can focus on meeting people where they are to win them.

>It takes serious dying to self to often relate to the unsaved, sometimes in the most obscure situations,

>Jesus could relate on all levels to all people and He has given us the grace and ability to do that for His purpose.

Prayer: Lord help me to be your witness today and not be religious in any way, but to be kind and reflective of your goodness and grace. Teach me your ways I pray. Amen.

November 6

Philippians 4:6 "Do not be anxious about anything, but in every situation, by prayer and petition, with thanksgiving, present your requests to God." NIV

> It is always a temptation to become anxious in challenging situations.
>
> It takes concerted effort and prayer not to become stressed, upset or anxious about situations. In fact, we have to make that decision.
>
> When we bring our request to Him it needs to be undergirded by faith, not fear or anxiety.

Prayer: Lord help me and teach me continually to not be anxious or reactionary to situations. Help me to not become emotional where I don't function by faith anymore and help me to present all these requests to you with prayer and thanksgiving. Amen.

November 7

Psalms 17:3 "You have tested my thoughts and examined my heart in the night. You have scrutinized me and found nothing wrong. I am determined not to sin in what I say." NLT

The Lord examines our hearts and motives and we ought to always keep them in check.

When, in relationship with the Lord, we allow Him to "scrutinize" our life we can always correct it and do what is right before the Lord.

It is a decision to put a watch in front of our mouth because we can sin in the things we say and be offense.

Prayer: Lord today I choose to follow you and love you and give you permission to examine my heart. Adjust my motives and correct me that I can grow and become all that you want me to be. It is you I love and you I want to please. Amen.

November 8

Matthew 7:1-2 "Do not judge others, and you will not be judged. For you will be treated as you treat others. The standard you use in judging is the standard by which you will be judged." NLT

Many of our obstacles and difficulties in life is a result of judging others.

It's not rocket science - having an opinion about someone else's heart or motivation is called judgement. Let's not do it.

If we can just focus on the Lord and leave Him to work with our brother or sister, we would be so much healthier. It is a trap of the enemy to try and make us focus or be mindful of other people's failings.

Prayer: Lord I ask you to help me keep my heart right that I will not judge or have opinions about other people's hearts or motivations. Help me to focus my heart on you and reflect you in all ways and have no preconceived ideas of other people. I praise you and bless you today. Amen.

November 9

Joshua 1:9 "This is my command—be strong and courageous! Do not be afraid or discouraged. For the Lord your God is with you wherever you go." NLT

In embarking on a new journey or going into the unknown, we need to have the courage of the Lord.

Fear is an entrapment to steal our faith and courage. It comes from the enemy.

The Lord "is" with us - where ever we go He is always there. He will never leave us.

Prayer: Lord I thank you as I start this new journey and embarking on territory unknown, I know you are with me and I will not be afraid and will not let the enemy put any apprehension in my heart. My trust is in you. Amen.

November 10

Isaiah 35:4 "Say to those with fearful hearts, "Be strong, and do not fear, for your God is coming to destroy your enemies. He is coming to save you." NLT

We cannot be ignorant of the fact that we have enemies, but the actual enemy is the devil who uses people and situations around us. He is actually the enemy.

The Lord will take care of the opposition.

He will always come through and we ought not be afraid or anxious.

Prayer: Lord I cast all my cares on you today. I throw my heart and self onto you that you will care for me and protect me today and rescue me from all my difficulties. I praise you. Amen.

November 11

2 Thessalonians 3:16 "Now may the Lord of peace himself give you his peace at all times and in every situation. The Lord be with you all." NLT

True peace is only found in God.

It is God's will for us to be at peace at all times regardless of what circumstance or situation we are in.

Situations change continually and we will not be moved by that - we will walk in His peace as a great gift.

Prayer: Lord I thank you for your peace that surpasses all understanding. And regardless of where I am and what I am going through I will walk in this great gift of peace you paid for so dearly. I praise you for it. Amen.

November 12

Number 11:1 "Now when the people complained, it displeased the Lord;" NKJV

It is very easy for us to complain, even when we have nothing to complain about - It is a bad habit and illustrates a lack of trust in the Lord.

Complaining really offends the Lord and we need to watch not to complain, but to develop a heart of praise and thanks giving.

The are always things and situations that we can focus on - I really believe we should count on what we have and not what we think we don't have.

Prayer: I praise you Lord that you are the alpha and omega, beginning and the end and that are you faithful. I ask that you give me a spirit of great thanks giving and joy as I really do love you and I am thankful. Amen.

November 13

1 Peter 3:15 "Instead, you must worship Christ as Lord of your life. And if someone asks about your Christian hope, always be ready to explain it." NLT

We ought not to wear people down but rather wait till they ask about it.

And be ready to testify to and glorify the Lord with our lives and what we say.

We put praising the Lord as the center of our daily lives because He is Lord of all.

Prayer: Lord I praise you today. You are the center of my universe and I am willingly anticipating for people to ask me about you so that I can tell them of your great love and salvation. Amen.

November 14

Hebrews 6:11 "Our great desire is that you will keep on loving others as long as life lasts, in order to make certain that what you hope for will come true." NLT

Christ genuinely expressed to the world, is certainly in how we love others.

Loving others many times takes more effort than we can accomplish on our own. We need His love to fill our hearts and that comes from waiting on Him.

This is an insurance for the future for ourselves and others, when we learn to continue to love others.

Prayer: Lord I ask you to fill me with your love today. Give me the ability to love even the unlovely people around me that I can express your greatness and love. You have loved me so much and it is only right that I should love all those around me. Amen.

November 15

Romans 6:22 "But now you are free from the power of sin and have become slaves of God. Now you do those things that lead to holiness and result in eternal life." NLT

> Free not to sin - we are from sin and also free to sin. It is a choice!
>
> We are not completely the Lord's and we start to develop habits and behavior that "lead" to holiness.
>
> This life and behavior results in eternal life.

Prayer: Lord I praise you for your salvation. Thank you that I am free from sin. Help me to walk in that path, developing a lifestyle that lead to holiness. I Praise you for it . Amen.

November 16

1 Timothy 1:17 "All honor and glory to God forever and ever! He is the eternal King, the unseen one who never dies; he alone is God." NLT

> We as His children should always be focusing on honoring Him on a daily basis.

> God is the one unstoppable eternal being.

> There is no other God but Him - we serve the one true God.

Prayer: Lord I praise you and honor you and lift you up today. Thank you for saving me and giving me this amazing gift of salvation. There is no one like you. You are the one and only true God. I praise you! Amen.

November 17

1 Thessalonians 4:13-14 "And now, dear brothers and sisters, we want you to know what will happen to the believers who have died so you will not grieve like people who have no hope. For since we believe that Jesus died and was raised to life again, we also believe that when Jesus returns, God will bring back with him the believers who have died." NLT

> We as his children always has this tremendous hope!
>
> Eternal life in Him is very real and all who believe in Him have this assurance.
>
> Even if we have lost someone and though it is sad, we have this assurance that we shall see them again all to soon.

Prayer: Lord I praise you that I know there is eternity waiting for all of us and as we are born again and redeemed we can be assured that we will go to be with you and those that have gone before us. I praise you for this blessed assurance. Amen.

November 18

Hebrews 12:1 "Therefore, since we are surrounded by such a huge crowd of witnesses to the life of faith, let us strip off every weight that slows us down, especially the sin that so easily trips us up. And let us run with endurance the race God has set before us." NLT

Our life is certainly a race - the beginning and end with a certain purpose.

There are those witnessing and watching our faith and how we respond to faith and grace.

Weights that slow us down are including sin, but not only sin. There are all kinds of fears and life's difficulties but we need to shake them all off.

Prayer: Lord I thank you for this faith and it grows inside of me as I know you. I want to finish this race with excellence, so I pray that you give me guidance and strength to do exactly that. Amen.

November 19

Ephesians 1:11 "Furthermore, because we are united with Christ, we have received an inheritance from God, for he chose us in advance, and he makes everything work out according to his plan." NLT

What a great joy that we are chosen by God - a great privilege!

We are united and become one with Him through this great salvation and can expect an inheritance, both natural and supernatural.

He makes everything work according to His plan - Even when things that happen to us seem so confusing and unusual they often work together for the plan.

Prayer: Lord I thank you that my life is in your hands and that you have chosen me. Even when things don't make sense to me I know you are at work with a whole plan. Amen.

November 20

Psalms 119:165 "Those who love your instructions have great peace and do not stumble." NLT

> More than just teaching - sometimes instructions can be adjustments or corrections.
>
> If we have the right attitude (love) towards these things from the Lord then we are assured this great peace.
>
> There is also an assurance when we follow God's ways we will not "stumble".

Prayer: Lord I thank you for this great promise of peace. I do love your instructions that you teach me in your ways. Thank you that I will not stumble, but follow you all the days of my life. Amen.

November 21

Isaiah 12:2 "See, God has come to save me. I will trust in him and not be afraid. The Lord God is my strength and my song; he has given me victory." NLT

> Often we are faced with a series crisis but we have this joy; He has come to save us.
>
> We will trust in Him and not be afraid - fear is a trap.
>
> The Lord is always our strength and has already given us the victory.

Prayer: Lord I praise you today that no matter what I face, you will be my helper and my savior. You are my victory and my strength. Amen.

November 22

Hebrews 13:15 "Through Jesus, therefore, let us continually offer to God a sacrifice of praise—the fruit of lips that openly profess his name." NIV

> Often praise takes effort because we don't always feel like it; it is a sacrifice.
>
> The fruit of our lips is actually our voicing it, the words that we speak.
>
> We "confess" His name and give glory to that name which is above every other name and we are not to be ashamed of it.

Prayer: Lord, today I praise you and with my heart and words I will continue to praise your name before man and angels. You are worthy and deserving of all my praise for your great love and salvation. Amen.

November 23

Philippians 4:8 "Finally, brothers and sisters, whatever is true, whatever is noble, whatever is right, whatever is pure, whatever is lovely, whatever is admirable—if anything is excellent or praiseworthy—think about such things." NIV

Even with so much negativity in the world, there is enough positive for us to focus our thoughts and hearts on.

It is beneficial to our natural health to focus on that which is good and pure.

It takes concerted effort to count on the things we do have and not focus on what we don't.

Prayer: Lord help me to focus all my thoughts on which is good, right, holy and pure in your sight that I will be full of joy today, knowing that you make all things work together for good. Amen.

November 24

Isaiah 55:11 "so is my word that goes out from my mouth: It will not return to me empty, but will accomplish what I desire and achieve the purpose for which I sent it." NIV

God's word is powerful and effective - whatever He said will be so.

Words that God has spoken doesn't return without accomplishing it's target - so if we have a promise we can depend upon it regardless of how long it takes.

God has a purpose for every word. He is the word that became flesh (John 1:1)

Prayer: Thank you Lord for your Word and the words you have spoken to me, through me and for me. I thank you that your words will not return void or become less than productive. Amen.

November 25

James 1:17 "Every good and perfect gift is from above, coming down from the Father of the heavenly lights, who does not change like shifting shadows." NIV

> Remembering today that all good things come from the Lord.
>
> The Father of Light - we keep walking in the light and we celebrate and enjoy who He is.
>
> God is not like man, up and down and undependable - He does not change!

Prayer: I praise you Lord that you are consistent and that I can depend upon you because you do not change. I thank you today for all the good gifts you give. Amen.

November 26

2 Corinthians 9:6 "Remember this: Whoever sows sparingly will also reap sparingly, and whoever sows generously will also reap generously." NIV

> Our seed determines our harvest.
>
> If what we have in our hand doesn't meet our need, it might just be our seed.
>
> We must keep sowing to have a harvest in due season.

Prayer: Lord help me to be free of fear of sowing my seed or giving generously so that I can reap bountifully. I praise you for all your provision. Amen.

November 27

Psalms 36:7 "How priceless is your unfailing love, O God! People take refuge in the shadow of your wings." NIV

God is not partial. No matter the status or position of man, whether in darkness or in light, He is kind to all.

His love is unfailing - nothing can separate us from this amazing love.

We can find refuge in Him at all times.

Prayer: Lord I thank you for your unfailing, wonderful love towards me and all those around me. Help me to remember and to walk in that love towards other people. Fill me with your love that I may be sustained in it. Amen.

November 28

Galatians 2:20 "I have been crucified with Christ and I no longer live, but Christ lives in me. The life I now live in the body, I live by faith in the Son of God, who loved me and gave himself for me." NIV

> Having been crucified with the Lord in our born again experience, we start our new life.
>
> Now, continually, Christ lives inside of us.
>
> By faith, we continue to walk in this natural man letting God walk with us now in this new life.

Prayer: Lord I praise you for this new life. The old man is dead and my new life has begun. Amen.

November 29

2 Corinthians 2:14 "But thanks be to God, who always leads us as captives in Christ's triumphal procession and uses us to spread the aroma of the knowledge of him everywhere." NIV

> We all give thanks to God because He is our victor.
>
> We are part of a procession that displays triumph - Jesus completed victory on calvary.
>
> A fragrance to be noted by all and all to give glory to Him for it.

Prayer: Lord I thank you for triumph and that I am part of the procession that the whole world may see. Let me be a fragrance of victory to all and help me to have that heart and attitude today. Amen.

November 30

Lamentations 3:22-23 "Because of the Lord's great love we are not consumed, for his compassions never fail. They are new every morning; great is your faithfulness." NIV

His love and compassion is new every morning.

Even though we as His people should need "consuming" of all God's anger, we have His compassion and mercy.

His great love - there is nothing that can match it on any level.

Prayer: Lord I rejoice in your great love and that it starts new and fresh every day with your compassion and grace. Thank you so much for your love and kindness. Help me to reflect that in everything I do today. Amen.

December 1

Hebrews 13:15 "Through Jesus, therefore, let us continually offer to God a sacrifice of praise—the fruit of our lips that openly profess his name." NIV

> It is through Jesus that we do everything.
>
> We must continue - not just sometimes but always - offer praise.
>
> It is a sacrifice when we don't feel like doing it but the fruit of our lips should be continually praising Him.

Prayer: Lord help me to be a light through praising your name daily even when I don't feel like it. I praise you now for your greatness. Amen.

December 2

Matthew 5:44-45 "But I tell you: Love your enemies and pray for those who persecute you, that you may be sons of your Father in heaven." NIV

Loving enemies can often be difficult, and usually only possible with God's help.

Just like Jesus prayed for those hammering the nails into His hands (Luke 23:34), we ought to pray for those that deliberately try to harm us.

This kind of love and response to people who are harsh and mean towards us exemplifies us as being God's children.

Prayer: Father, I acknowledge that in my own strength I cannot love people that are harmful to me, and ask You to fill me with Your love for them. Amen.

December 3

Galatians 3:26 "By faith in Christ you are in direct relationship with God." MSG

> Abraham was counted righteous by faith - not by actions, blood sacrifice or any other deed - by faith!
>
> Relationship is a two way street and a delightful adventure for those that 'seek' and pursue Him!
>
> What a privilege - to be so closely connected with God - though our Lord Jesus!

Prayer: Lord I thank you for this great salvation and Your great unfailing love. I praise you today for all Your greatness! Amen.

December 4

Romans 14:17 "For the kingdom of God is not a matter of eating and drinking, but of righteousness, peace and joy in the Holy Spirit," NIV

> We are part of this Kingdom - a kingdom that belongs solely to the Lord.
>
> This kingdom is righteousness - continuing in right relationship with God the Father.
>
> This kingdom always consists of peace and joy.

Prayer: Father help me to live and walk continually in this kingdom that I can experience this joy and peace and reflect you to the world. Amen.

December 5

1 Timothy 6:20-21 "Timothy, guard what has been entrusted to your care. Turn away from godless chatter and the opposing ideas of what is falsely called knowledge, which some have professed and in so doing have departed from the faith." NIV

We must protect what the Lord entrust us with, the truth revelation and his mandate to us individually.

"Godless chatter" can become a death trap in our journey, and it needs to be avoided.

Debating worldly standard of knowledge can injure our faith and we need to soak ourselves in His Word.

Prayer: Father, help me to watch and be careful not to be involved in idle talk and fruitless chatter. I love you Lord and desire that my talk reflect that continually. Amen.

December 6

1 John 1:7 "But if we walk in the light, as he is in the light, we have fellowship with one another, and the blood of Jesus, his Son, purifies us from all sin." NIV

Walking in the light - means to follow His way and truth regardless of how it seems at the time.

Those that walk in the light and follow this way immediately have common fellowship and we are able to recognize those that are like heart and faith.

Walking in the light ensures the full value of His blood purifying us of all sin at all times.

Prayer: Lord help me to walk in the light daily light of your truth so I can recognize my brethren and enjoy the fullness of this salvation. I praise you today as you are the Lord of light. Amen.

December 7

Philippians 2:12-13 "Therefore, my dear friends, as you have always obeyed—not only in my presence, but now much more in my absence—continue to work out your salvation with fear and trembling, for it is God who works in you to will and to act in order to fulfill his good purpose." NIV

Working out our salvation is a daily journey of relationship with Him. Growing and learning from Him.

"fear and trembling" is an attitude of reverence, understanding the full severity of this salvation and we ought to take this salvation seriously.

God is working to create in us the right nature and behavior according to His purpose.

Prayer: Father please continue working in me that your nature can be seen as I cling to you today. You are my Lord and the love of my life. Amen.

December 8

Philippians 2:14-15 "Do everything without complaining or arguing, so that you may become blameless and pure, children of God without fault in a warped and crooked generation. Then you will shine among them like stars in the sky." NIV

> Whining does not produce Christ-like life. It is so easy for us to murmur - let's resist it!
>
> The purpose of this attitude is to become blameless and pure so that we can "shine like stars".
>
> Through these things we can make a difference and be a testimony to the world.

Prayer: Lord, help me to be a "shining star" by not arguing or being a complainer and always having a good, godly attitude. I realize that I am weak and cannot do this in my own strength. Amen.

December 9

Psalm 119:105 "By your words I can see where I'm going; they throw abeam of light on my dark path. I've committed myself and I'll never turn back from living by your righteous order." MSG

> Thank God for His written Word - the most wonderful gift - the Bible. Jesus applied the written Word in the wilderness in His struggle against the devil.
>
> His word is in every way is like a light or flashlight on our journey.
>
> His written and spoken Word give us an 'order' to live by.

Prayer: Thank you, Father, for Your Word, both written and spoken. Give me a hunger for Your Word and ability to remember it when in need. Amen.

December 10

Isaiah 26:3 "You will keep in perfect peace those whose minds are steadfast, because they trust in you." NIV

> There is no peace that compares to the peace that the Lord gives.
>
> Life has so many challenges and difficulties but we have joy and peace that comes from the Lord only, even while we are in the storm.
>
> We have to focus our minds on Him and His Word. All thoughts need to be taken captive and directed on Him.

Prayer: Lord I ask you today to take my mind and all my thoughts captive that I may focus on you only. Help me to walk in your perfect peace, day and night, no matter what troubles I go through. I praise you for it. In Jesus name. Amen.

December 11

Romans 13:10 "Love does no harm to a neighbor. Therefore love is the fulfillment of the law." NIV

> Christianity 101 - there is nothing that surpasses the law of love!
>
> All real and true love has its origin in God and it is pure and unadulterated.
>
> When we function in this love, it covers absolutely every law and principle of christianity.

Prayer: Lord, thank you for your love for me. Fill me with it today and every day that I can be a vessel and an instrument of your love. I praise you and worship you today as you are the God of love. Amen.

December 12

James 3:13 "Who is wise and understanding among you? Let them show it by their good life, by deeds done in the humility that comes from wisdom." NIV

Wisdom is to be sought after according to the Song of Solomon and it is more than just knowledge, it is the application of knowledge and understanding.

Good life is exemplary, and deeds that are seen by man display clearly God's involvement in our lives.

Humility - the attitude of our hearts which is derived from wisdom, attracts God as He lifts up the humble.

Prayer: Lord I desire and pursue your wisdom. I ask you to help me to become wise that I can really be a blessing to other people and that they can see through my deeds, your love and greatness today. Amen.

December 13

Mark 9:23 "'If you can"?' said Jesus. 'Everything is possible for one who believes.' NIV

There is absolutely no limit! Jesus said "everything".

The key or condition is for us to believe - why would that be? Because our faith is continually attacked with the goal of putting us in fear and doubt.

The volume of faith is less important than the purity of it. And the purity is strengthened and advanced by dwelling in and on the Word continually.

Prayer: Lord I do believe. Help my fear and unbelief today that I will believe for the things that seem impossible to me. I praise you that you are a mighty God and that there is no limit to what you can and will do. Amen.

December 14

1 Peter 1:15-16 "But just as he who called you is holy, so be holy in all you do; for it is written: 'Be holy, because I am holy.'" NIV

> Holiness is the presence of God rather than the sinlessness that we thought it once was. (God was holy before there ever was sin)
>
> When we dwell in His presence, then sin automatically is no where to be found because our appetites and behaviors changes naturally.
>
> So rather than fighting sin, we pursue holiness and it is visible in all we do!

Prayer: Lord I thank you for your salvation. I desire to be holy as you are holy; fill me with your presence so that there is no room for anything that is evil or sinful in my life. Fill me up with you Holy Spirit today I pray in Jesus' name. Amen.

December 15

1 Thessalonians 5:24 "The one who calls you is faithful, and he will do it." NIV

God calls us - many are called but few are chosen. And as you read this today it is clear that you are a chosen one, saved by His grace.

He certainly is more than just faithful. There is nothing to compare to His faithfulness. We can rely on Him.

The promise is "He will do it". We can count on it today.

Prayer: Lord I thank you for saving me, for calling me and for choosing me. I ask you Lord to give me the confidence, as you are faithful, to expect you to do it and to complete the work you have begun in me. Amen.

December 16

John 15:7 "If you remain in me and my words remain in you, ask whatever you wish, and it will be done for you." NIV

"Remaining in Him" indicates that though we are saved and born again, there is an effort we must make to stay continually in relationship with Him.

The only way He can remain in us, is if we maintain our relationship with Him - and that is by spending time with Him. Waiting on Him, listening to Him and talking to Him daily.

"Ask whatever you wish" has a very clear indication that there is no limit. When we ask, it will be given to us. So let us put that in practice today.

Prayer: Lord I do ask clearly today what I desire and wish. I thank you for all the answered prayers in my life already. Clearly you are a God that answers prayers and I praise you for it today. Amen.

December 17

Romans 3:21 "But now apart from the law the righteousness of God has been made known, to which the Law and the Prophets testify." NIV

> Righteousness - to be in right standing with God. What a glorious concept!
>
> This righteousness is separate to all law and requirements - It comes from grace and mercy.
>
> Even the law and the prophets pointed to this amazing salvation; that we are made right with God through His mercy when we accept Him.

Prayer: Lord I am overwhelmed by this great salvation today and that you would have mercy on me while I was yet a sinner. I praise you for your goodness and your love towards me. Amen.

December 18

Acts 1:7 "He said to them: 'It is not for you to know the times or dates the Father has set by his own authority." NIV

Our times and seasons are certainly in God's hands; each one of us individually and us collectively.

Jesus said it is not for us to know some of the details of the times - we are to trust Him and know that He is completely in control.

God sets the times and season by His authority and reveals it through His kindness and revelation when He chooses,

Prayer: Lord I thank you that you are sovereign and all is in your control. Though I do not know what tomorrow holds or what to expect, I know that I am safe in your hands. These things are under your authority and control. I praise you for you greatness today. Amen.

December 19

Ephesians 4:2 "Be completely humble and gentle; be patient, bearing with one another in love. Make every effort to keep the unity of the Spirit through the bond of peace." NIV

> We need to pursue a humble heart and attitude - not thinking more about ourselves than we ought to.
>
> Being patient is a constant virtue that helps us to interact and be christ-like with each other.
>
> "Bearing" is tolerating and being gracious to other people so that we can have unity and christ-likeness amongst ourselves.

Prayer: Lord I pray that you create in me a clean and contrite heart and help me to have a humble spirit to do these things, to be patient and interact with my brethren and people around me with gentleness and love. Amen.

December 20

Isaiah 30:18 "Yet the Lord longs to be gracious to you; he rises to show you compassion. For the Lord is a God of justice. Blessed are all who wait for him!" NIV

> It is the nature and heart of God that wants to show us kindness and grace. He picks us up in the worst of circumstances.
>
> He is a God of justice and He measures what is right - not the opinion of man, but to His own holiness.
>
> We are blessed when we wait on Him. Sometimes He seems slow but His time is always perfect.

Prayer: Lord I thank you that you long to show me grace and want to be kind to me. I am grateful for your grace and your justice. Today I purpose in my heart to look to you as my entire source of life. Amen.

December 21

Psalms 32:8 "I will instruct you and teach you in the way you should go; I will counsel you and watch over you." NIV

What an amazing promise - the Lord's guidance. So often we just don't know what to do and we are not sure of the next step or the right response to a situation.

The counsel of the Lord is wise and we ought to take time to listen and wait on Him for it.

In every situation we should remember that He is watching over us.

Prayer: Lord I thank you today for your instruction and guidance. Help me to always be mindful of your guidance and to take time to wait on you for it. Amen.

December 22

Isaiah 40:31 "but those who hope in the Lord will renew their strength. They will soar on wings like eagles; they will run and not grow weary, they will walk and not be faint." NIV

> Waiting on the Lord is an attitude of focussing on, depending and relying on the Lord - being mindful of Him throughout the day.
>
> Our strength needs to be renewed often as we fight in a battle.
>
> We will not fail or "faint" as we renew our strength and allow the Lord to raise us up and make us strong.

Prayer: Lord I commit my way, my heart and life to you. I thank you that you will renew my strength and when I am weak you are my strength and my helper. Amen.

December 23

Matthew 6:14-15 "For if you forgive men their trespasses, your heavenly Father will also forgive you. But if you do not forgive men their trespasses, neither will your Father forgive your trespasses." NKJV

Forgiveness is essential to our spiritual heath and well being. We cannot afford to entertain any unforgiveness of any nature or any size.

We are assured that God will not hold sins against us if we truly forgive from our hearts.

We are tested daily in this matter and the way to overcome unforgiveness is to never start. The moment someone hurts or offends us we must forgive them instantly, even before they ask.

Prayer: Lord help me to live a life with forgiveness and continually be a blessing to others through my heart and attitude, Hold nothing against anyone that offends or hurts me. Amen.

December 24

1 Peter 1:7-9 "These have come so that the proven genuineness of your faith—of greater worth than gold, which perishes even though refined by fire—may result in praise, glory and honor when Jesus Christ is revealed. Though you have not seen him, you love him; and even though you do not see him now, you believe in him and are filled with an inexpressible and glorious joy, for you are receiving the end result of your faith, the salvation of your souls." NIV

There is no question that our faith is under constant trial and testing and even under attack.

The testing of our faith is to accomplish the refining thereof and to bring us to higher levels.

We are not to see testing or trials of our faith as negative but rather as a life-giving source and positive things for the future.

Prayer: Lord help me to have the right attitude towards the testing of my faith. Help me not to give up but rather recognize when my faith is being tested and to rejoice knowing that you are perfecting your purpose in me. Amen.

December 25

Isaiah 9:6 "For unto us a Child is born, Unto us a Son is given; And the government will be upon His shoulder. And His name will be called Wonderful, Counselor, Mighty God, Everlasting Father, Prince of Peace." NKJV

For us - and me personally - a child is born to be a savior and a helper. God knew and cared about me personally before the world began.

And He would be great - counselor, mighty God. This is my Jesus that has taken my place and have given me the right to call Him Lord, Master and Father.

What a day of rejoicing, that Jesus has come into this world just for me and those that have been saved.

Prayer: Lord I rejoice today and thank you that you came and are willing to die for me. Willing to walk for 33 years to initiate and orchestrate a salvation that is so great and so wonderful. I am so deeply grateful. I praise you for it today. Amen.

December 26

2 Corinthians 4:8-10 "We are hard-pressed on every side, yet not crushed; we are perplexed, but not in despair; persecuted, but not forsaken; struck down, but not destroyed— always carrying about in the body the dying of the Lord Jesus, that the life of Jesus also may be manifested in our body." NKJV

> There is no question that there are times in our lives that we go through hard times and can feel that it is coming from all angels.
>
> Even though we go through hard times we are not pressed down completely and we shouldn't lose hope or become full of despair.
>
> And we know that through this we know we are getting stronger because He is our strength when we are weak.

Prayer: Lord I thank you that you are my strength. Through all my challenges and storms you are my helper and I thank you that you are perfecting me for your purpose and plan. Amen.

December 27

Philippians 4:17 "Not that I am looking for a gift, but I am looking for what may be credited to your account." NIV

> The support of the ministry is God's way and He promises a serious reward. (Mark 10:29-30)
>
> Giving is not so that the church or ministry may receive but they it may be 'credited to our account.'
>
> We give generously to reap a generous reward and we give joyfully as the Lord loves a cheerful giver.

Prayer: Lord, I give my tithe and offerings willingly and gladly. Lead me daily to give in obedience to You and help me to expect and see a return as You promised. Amen.

December 28

Psalms 100:2 "Serve the Lord with gladness; Come before His presence with singing." NKJV

> We follow and serve the Lord with "gladness" - we are joyous and it is a privilege to know and serve our mighty Lord.
>
> We make a conscious effort and habit to focus on serving God and we come into His presence with praise on a daily basis.
>
> It is a lifestyle and habit that we are forming to be joyous and full of praise no matter what the circumstances are.

Prayer: Lord I thank you that today no matter what I go through or whatever happens my trust and hope can be in you. I look to you for my strengthening and my help. I praise and worship you today. Amen.

December 29

Proverbs 3:5-6 "Trust in the Lord with all your heart, And lean not on your own understanding; In all your ways acknowledge Him, And He shall direct your paths." NKJV

> We are not to trust God with our minds because our minds are often in turmoil.
>
> We have to trust Him with our hearts and not try to think things through.
>
> When we acknowledge Him and give Him complete preeminence then He directs our paths and no matter what things look like, He is in control of our destiny and paths.

Prayer: I praise you Lord as I lean, with my whole heart, unto you and not on my own understanding. You will direct my paths and orchestrate my life no matter how things appear to me. I praise you for it. Amen.

December 30

John 14:1 "Let not your heart be troubled; you believe in God, believe also in Me." NKJV

> We have to work at not letting our hearts be anxious or "troubled".
>
> It is not the Lord's desire or God's heart for us to be stressed about anything - We trust God and Jesus asks us to trust Him too.
>
> Trusting Him - If we saw and understood everything God is doing we wouldn't need to trust Him!

Prayer: Lord I choose today to trust you completely and not allow my heart to be troubled. Help me to overcome any anxiety or stress in my life today. Amen.

December 31

Isaiah 50:7 "For the Lord God will help Me; Therefore I will not be disgraced; Therefore I have set My face like a flint, And I know that I will not be ashamed." NKJV

We have knowledge that God will help us regardless of how unworthy we might feel - because He is faithful!

I will not be ashamed or embarrassed.

I will set my face like a "flint" means to be resolute and not be moved by my circumstances or embarrassed. The Lord is my strength.

Prayer: I praise you today Lord because I know you will help me and I will be confident in your grace and your goodness and your strength. Not my own strength or my worthiness, but your greatness. Amen.

LIFEWORDS
A Prophetic Life Daily Devotional

by Ed Traut

Made in the USA
Lexington, KY
19 May 2014